Festival

Christmas Annual 2024

This Christmas annual belongs to:

Name/Ainm/Nazwa/Ім'я:

Age/Aois/Wiek/Вік:

School/Scoil/Szkoła/Школа:

educate.ie

Design and Layout: Karyn Moynihan

Cover Design: Kieran O'Donoghue

Illustrations: Emma Trithart/Bright Agency

Photographs: Adobe Stock, Alamy, Cheer Sport Ireland, Shutterstock

ISBN: 978-1-916832-75-6

Printed in Ireland by Walsh Colour Print, Castleisland, Co. Kerry.

www.educate.ie

Contents

Welcome to *Festival* 2024!

Carols on the radio, twinkly lights everywhere, and of course annuals arriving at school ... it must be Christmas! Turn the pages to find the very best of puzzles, recipes, jokes, articles and more to brighten up these winter days.

Why not get started by checking out our 2024 Quiz on page 5 to see how much you remember from the past year of news and events?

Starting on page 24, you can read about this year's big anniversaries, including *Riverdance* and the Wild Atlantic Way.

Have you got all the ingredients you need to try our recipe for Jelly Wreath Cake on page 12?

Or turn to page 18, where you can enjoy a brand-new Christmas story written by this year's writing competition winner! Check it out and get thinking about your own story ideas ... could you be next year's *Festival* writing competition winner, and see your work published?

We hope you will enjoy *Festival* 2024, which we have filled with as much joy and entertainment as we could find!

From all of us here at the Christmas Annual offices, have a wonderful time celebrating the season, spending time with your family and perhaps enjoying a few gifts or special treats! We wish you a merry one!

The *Festival* Team

2024 Quiz

How much do you remember from the past year?

See how many questions you can answer about the year's news, sport, TV, music and celebrities!

1. 2024 was the Chinese Year of the what?
2. What company was announced as the new sponsor of the Irish men's soccer team in March 2024?
3. The 2024 Olympics took place in which European country?
4. Leo Varadkar stepped down as Ireland's Taoiseach in April 2024. Who replaced him as Taoiseach and as leader of the Fine Gael Party?
5. Which American football team beat the San Francisco 49ers to win the 2024 Super Bowl?
6. What is the name of singer Taylor Swift's boyfriend, who played on the winning Super Bowl team?
7. What was the name of the new album released by Taylor Swift in April 2024?
8. What popular animated 2004 Christmas film, about a boy's extraordinary train ride to the North Pole, turned 20 years old in 2024?
9. What popular children's book, about a character with 'terrible tusks, terrible claws, and terrible teeth in his terrible jaws', turned 25 years old in 2024?
10. Who won the 2024 series of RTÉ's *Dancing with the Stars*?
11. What singer of songs such as 'Dance the Night' and 'Houdini' won the Pop Act award at the 2024 Brit Awards?
12. What Australian cartoon about a family of dogs including Bingo, Bandit and Chilli released a special long episode in 2024, and brought its touring stage show to the Olympia Theatre in Dublin?
13. What New Zealand rugby player signed a contract to play for Leinster for the 2024/25 season?
14. What pop singer became father to baby Madison in April 2024?
15. What British TV duo wrapped up their Saturday night TV show in 2024 after 20 seasons?
16. Can you name the 2024 RTÉ sports documentary where ten boys aged 12–14 take part in training and learn more about themselves with presenter and rugby player Jordan Conroy?

17. What Irish actor was announced as the new face of the brand Versace in 2024?
18. Who became the youngest person ever to win two Oscars this year, receiving an award for the song 'What Was I Made For?', having previously won in 2022 for the song 'No Time to Die'?
19. In 2024, Ireland introduced a returns system for drink bottles and cans. What deposit fee do shoppers have to pay per drinks container, which they can only get back if the empty, cleaned container is returned after use?
20. In 2024, it was announced that a famous board game would be adapted into a film. Can you name the board game?
21. In 2024, Ireland unveiled its first fully roofed street! A busy street called Monck Street got a fully retractable roof costing more than €1.5 million. What county is it in?
22. What former Irish president celebrated their 80th birthday in 2024?
23. In 2024, the Leinster rugby team lost the European Rugby Champions Cup final for the third year in a row. What team won?
24. True or false: Manchester City won the 2024 FA Cup final.

Answers on page 77

2024's Zaniest News!

It has certainly been a busy year, so amongst all the usual stories of sports wins, celebrity happenings and so on in the news, you might have missed these zany, crazy, amazing, sometimes heart-warming, and often unbelievable, 2024 moments!

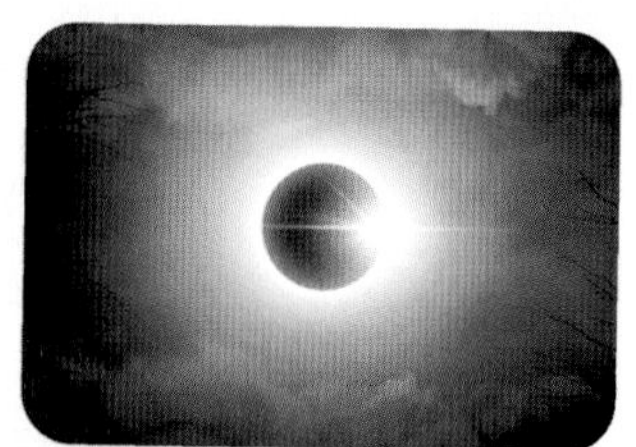

New Yorker Patrick Moriarty started teaching Science in 1978. When his students studied eclipses, he told them about one that would pass near their town on 8 April 2024 and promised them they could get together to witness it ... even though it would not be happening for almost five decades. Two years ago, as the eclipse was finally getting close, Moriarty, then aged 66, set up a Facebook event to try to find his former students and invite them to watch the eclipse with him. He ordered pizza for the event and bought 130 pairs of eclipse glasses. Word spread and sure enough, on 8 April, almost 100 of Moriarty's former students showed up to watch the eclipse with him in his garden in Rochester, New York!

In 2024, Liverpudlian John Alfred Tinniswood, aged 111, was confirmed to be the world's oldest man by Guinness World Records. The retired accountant said the secret to his long life is luck, moderation (he never smokes and rarely drinks), and eating fish and chips on a Friday!

You may wish you lived in Detroit, Michigan, USA, when you hear this next zany news story. In March 2024, it rained marshmallows in Catalpa Oaks County Park in Southfield, Detroit. A helicopter dropped 15,000 marshmallows to hundreds of waiting children in an event known as the annual Great Marshmallow Drop! The helicopter made drops in four different passes, with kids organised in different areas by age group, for safety. We were also delighted to read that there was a dedicated marshmallow drop for kids with additional needs, as it's very important to include everyone in the community when we organise events. Alas, though they are delicious, the Great Drop marshmallows do land on open grass, so it's recommended not to eat them. Instead, children collect them up and exchange them for party bags containing sweets, a colouring book and an entry ticket to a local water park.

Did you know that Paris has a special race celebrating the waiters and waitresses of the city? 2024's winners were Pauline Van Wymeersch and Samy Lamrous. Those taking part balance a tray with a croissant, a coffee cup and a glass of water as they run two kilometres through the streets of Paris. The first race was in 1914. In recent years the race did not take place, but it was resurrected this year for the first time since 2010, to celebrate another sporting event coming to the city – namely the summer Olympic Games in July.

In New South Wales in Australia, commuters at a train station were surprised to see a racehorse queuing on the platform! The Transport Authority shared footage online of Warwick Farm Station on 5 April, where an escaped racehorse is standing behind the yellow line, waiting for his train. The Transport Authority said it was just horseplay! Groan.

Spot the Difference 1

There are six small differences between these two pictures.
Can you find all of them?

Answers on page 77

Calm Christmas Colouring

Have you heard of mindfulness before? Mindfulness is all about paying attention to one thing at a time. It's especially helpful at times such as Christmas, when life can get busy and loud! One simple way to be mindful is to spend some time colouring in pictures. Don't just get scribbling, though – make sure you use the following tips to really chill out.

- Choose a quiet, comfy space to spend some time by yourself. Maybe wrap yourself up with blankets and cushions or play some nice music at a low volume.
- Imagine the sounds, smells, details or feelings in your Christmas pictures. What do the Christmas cookies smell like? What is wrapped up in the Christmas gift boxes?
- Pay attention to your breathing as you work. Every time you choose a new part of your picture to colour, take a big deep breath in through your nose and let it out slowly through your mouth.

We hope you enjoy *Festival*'s selection of Christmas colouring this year!

Merry and Bright

Synonym Rolls!

A synonym is a word or phrase that has almost exactly the same meaning as another word or phrase, for example, 'begin' and 'start'.

Cinnamon = a delicious spice!

Cinnamon rolls = delicious doughy treats made with cinnamon, butter and icing, often eaten around Christmas time.

Synonym rolls = a delicious word challenge for you to play this Christmas!

Each of the synonym rolls below has a partner with a similar meaning. See if you can match them up.

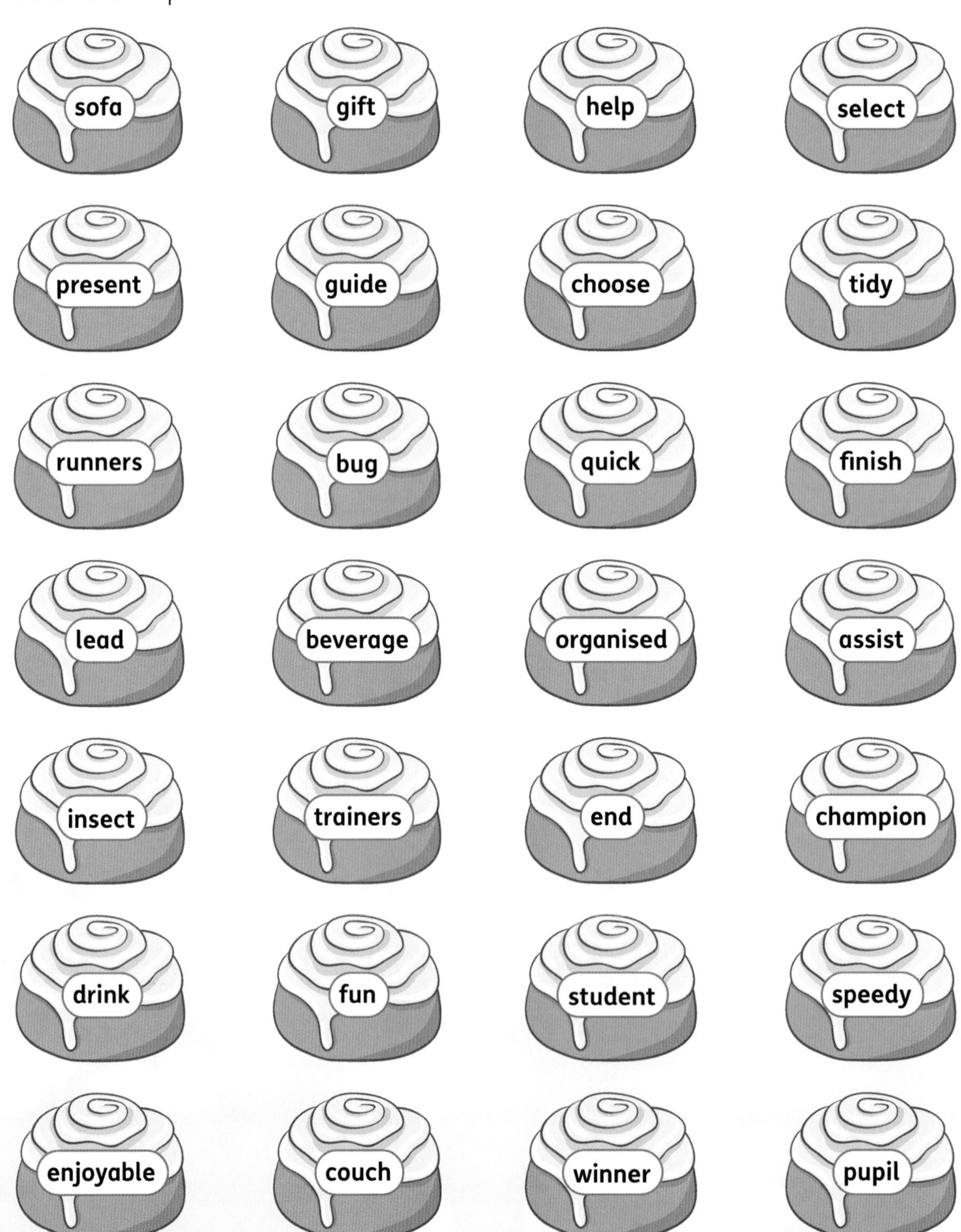

Answers on page 77

Synonym Rolls as Gaeilge!

Freagraí ar leathanach 77

Recipe: Jelly Wreath Cake

Fancy impressing everyone at home by offering to make a delicious Christmas dessert? Follow these simple steps and with a little time and effort, you will have a seriously fun food to enjoy!

You will need:

- 3 eggs
- 85 g caster sugar
- 85 g self-raising flour
- Strawberry or raspberry jam
- 125 ml fresh cream
- Block of strawberry or raspberry jelly
- Desiccated coconut

Equipment:

- Weighing scales
- Stand mixer or whisk
- Bowls
- Sieve
- Ring tin (also known as a savarin mould)
- Wire rack
- Knives and spoons
- Parchment paper
- Cling film

Be safe!

Ask an adult for help with using the oven and pouring boiling water.

What to do:

1. Begin by weighing and measuring out ingredients.
2. Preheat the oven to 160 degrees (fan-assisted) or gas mark 3.
3. Line the ring tin with parchment paper.
4. Crack three eggs into a mixing bowl and beat, adding caster sugar a little at a time. The mixture should be light and have air bubbles.
5. Sieve in self-raising flour and fold the mixture together.
6. Place the mixture in the lined ring tin and bake for 20–25 minutes. When the cake is ready, it will be a golden colour and will spring back when pressed.
7. Remove the cake from the tin and leave to cool on a wire rack.
8. Whip cream.
9. While the cake is cooling, boil a kettle of water and prepare the jelly according to the instructions on the packet, but do not allow to fully set.
10. Slice the cake in half. Spread one side with jam and the other with cream, then sandwich together.
11. Clean the ring tin and pour in the jelly, then place the cake in on top, pressing down so the jelly spreads up the sides of the tin to surround the sponge cake.
12. Cover the cake, still in its tin, with cling film and place in the fridge to set. This will take three or four hours.
13. When the cake has set, remove it from the tin and place on a plate (jelly side up!).
14. If you would like a snowy wreath, sprinkle the cake with desiccated coconut.
15. Serve and enjoy!

Sudoku 1

Have you played sudoku before? Sudoku is a game involving the numbers 1–9.

Each number should appear only once in each small square, and once in each line – both in columns up and down, and in rows from side to side!

Use these rules to work out the missing numbers!

TIPS AND TRICKS

- ✓ **Start with a row or column that already has a good few numbers filled in.**
- ✓ **Figure out which numbers between 1 and 9 are missing and start to work out where they might go.**
- ✓ **If you get stuck, try a different row or square!**

	2		5			7		
1		8	4	2	7			
7					9		1	
		5						4
2	6						5	1
9						3		
	8		9					3
			1	7	8	5		6
		7			5		4	

Answers on page 77

Tráth na gCeist: Cé hIad?

1. Is aisteoir Éireannach í. Rugadh í i nGaillimh i mí Eanáir 1987. Tháinig cáil uirthi i 2018 nuair a bhí ról aici i *Derry Girls*. Tá sí ar an gclár Netflix *Bridgerton*. Cé hí?

2. Is peileadóir é. Rugadh é i Sasana i mí an Mheithimh 2003. Thosaigh sé ag imirt leis an acadamh i Birmingham City nuair a bhí sé ocht mbliana d'aois. Is é an t-imreoir is óige riamh chun scór a fháil do Shasana i gcraobhchomórtas Eorpach UEFA. Bhog sé go Real Madrid i 2023. Cé hé?

3. Is cantóir agus aisteoir í. Rugadh í i Florida i mí an Mheithimh 1993. Thosaigh sí amach ag obair ar an gclár *Victorious*. Tá deartháir cáiliúil aici darbh ainm Frankie. Tá cáil ar a hamhráin 'Thank U, Next' agus '7 Rings'. Cé hí?

4. Is cruthaitheoir ábhair YouTube agus Twitch é. Rugadh é i gcathair Nua Eabhrac i mí na Nollag 2001. Rinneadh mearscaipeadh ar a shraith fhíseáin *Ding Dong Ditch*. Cé hé?

5. Is imreoir dairteanna é. Rugadh é i Sasana i mí Eanáir 2007. Is é 'The Nuke' an leasainm atá aige. Bhuaigh sé an Premier League dairteanna i mí Bealtaine 2024. Cé hé?

Freagraí ar leathanach 77

Celebrity Profile

Jürgen Klopp

Born: 16 June 1967
From: Stuttgart, Germany
Height: 6 ft 3"
Star sign: Gemini

Former Liverpool manager Jürgen Klopp is considered to be one of the best football managers in the world, famous for his pressing and counter-pressing tactics.

Klopp was a player until 2001. Starting out his career as a striker before becoming a defender, he spent most of his playing years with German club Mainz 05. Klopp was Mainz 05's record goalscorer, with 56 goals in total.

When Klopp retired from play, he became the club's manager, and within three years they were promoted to Germany's Bundesliga despite having the smallest budget and smallest stadium in the league. They had some successes, but their promotion did not last, and they suffered relegation in the 2006/07 season.

In 2008, Klopp resigned and moved to Borussia Dortmund. Dortmund had some record-breaking seasons under Klopp. For example, in 2011, his squad were the youngest-ever side to win the Bundesliga. They successfully defended the title the following season, achieving a record 81 points.

Klopp stayed with Dortmund until 2015, when he signed a three-year deal to join the team where he would really make his name: Liverpool.

Liverpool Under Klopp

- UEFA Champions League finalists 2018 and 2022
- UEFA Champions League winners 2019
- Second-place finish in the 2018–9 Premier League, registering 97 points
- UEFA Super Cup winners 2019
- FIFA Club World Cup winners 2019
- Premier League winners 2019–20
- EFL Cup winners 2022
- FA Cup winners 2022
- EFL Cup winners 2024
- A string of records for unbeaten runs in domestic and international leagues
- Maintaining a win rate of more than 60%

Klopp won the FIFA Coach of the Year awards in 2019 and 2020. He has also variously been named BBC Sports Coach of the Year, LMA Manager of the Year, German Football Manager of the Year and World Soccer Awards Manager of the Year. He has been a Premier League Manager of the Month on ten occasions. He was awarded the Freedom of the City of Liverpool in 2022.

Klopp is well loved at Anfield. Between 2015 and 2020, he made Liverpool the champions of English, European and world football. He ended the Reds' 30-year wait for a league title in 2020 when they secured the top spot in the Premier League.

On 26 January 2024, Klopp announced that he would leave Liverpool and take a break from football management at the end of the 2023/24 season. He leaves behind some heartbroken fans!

Interesting Facts

✓ Klopp's middle name is Norbert.

✓ At the 2019 FIFA Awards Ceremony, Klopp announced that he had signed up for the Common Goals fund, and would be donating 1% of his salary to a charity that funds organisations that use football to tackle social issues.

✓ Klopp has appeared in ads for Puma, Snickers and Opel, amongst others. In 2020, he signed a personal endorsement deal with Adidas.

Klopp in Quotes

- On being better as a manager than as a player: 'I had fourth division feet and a first division head.'
- On the claim that Borussia Dortmund's performances improved after he announced he was leaving: 'If I'd known, I would have announced it at the beginning of the season.'
- 'The best football is always about expression of emotion.'

Festival **Christmas Writing Competition Winner:**

No Glow

by Caroline Foley, St Anne's National School, Shankill, Dublin 18

It was Christmas Eve when disaster struck. It was a foggy, stormy night and children all around the world were hanging up their stockings and tucking up in bed, dreaming sweet dreams of sugarplums and candy canes. But at the North Pole, there was chaos. You may think that this was normal for Christmas Eve, but this year was especially bad, because, for the first time, Rudolph's nose had stopped glowing!

While the worker elves ran around in distress, Santa and the head elves held an emergency meeting.

'SANTA, WHAT ARE WE GOING TO DO! IT'S THE FOGGIEST CHRISTMAS EVE SINCE YOU GAVE RUDOLPH THE JOB IN THE FIRST PLACE!' cried the Head Elf of Present Wrapping, who everyone called Shouty, because, well, he was very shouty.

'Shouty please, you'll just cause more panic with all that yelling,' grumbled Santa.

'With all due respect, sir,' said Baubles, Head of Toy Management, 'things couldn't be more chaotic. All of my elves are a mess, either so worried that they can't do anything but sit down and stare at the ground, or so desperate for answers that they are frenzying themselves into a mob.'

The elves started arguing and complaining about poor management. Santa put his head in his hands.

'I'm getting too old for this,' Santa sighed. 'Does anyone have a good idea?'

One elf, who had been silent so far, finally spoke up. 'I have an idea, Santa,' she said. Then she realised she had spoken too quietly and shouted, 'I HAVE AN IDEA, SANTA!'

Everyone stopped fighting and stared.

'Who said that?' asked Santa. He adjusted his glasses. 'Oh, Sparky! Good to see you! I thought you had died!'

'Err, no sir. I'm Pudding, Head of Reindeer Care,' said Pudding.

'Bother, sorry dear, age is really taking its toll on me. You said you had an idea?' Santa replied.

'Yes, Santa,' chirped Pudding, 'I noticed that Rudolph has been acting a bit distant with the other reindeer for a while now, and I think that the brightness of his nose might have something to do with the brightness of his mood.'

'Interesting,' mused Santa.

'Oh, please,' scoffed Baubles, 'you don't seriously believe her, do you?'

'If things are really as bad as you claim, Baubles, then I'm willing to try anything,' said Santa.

Santa and the head elves set off for the reindeer stables. As Santa followed her through to Rudolph's stall, Pudding felt the most nervous she had in her entire life. She knew if she messed this up, she would be a laughing stock amongst the elves forever. But, if she was right, she would be a hero.

'We're here, Santa,' she squeaked as they arrived outside of Rudolph's stall. Rudolph looked very sad indeed, curled up in the corner with his head down. And worst of all was his nose, which was dark.

'My poor boy,' sobbed Santa. 'My, poor, poor, boy.'

Pudding patted Santa tentatively on the back. 'I'm sure this is very upsetting for you Santa, but if we're going to cheer Rudolph up, we need to act happy,' she advised.

'Right,' said Santa, pulling himself together impressively quickly. 'I need to be strong, for him.'

Santa walked into the stall and sat down beside Rudolph. He produced a handful of candy canes from who knows where and offered them to the sad reindeer. Rudolph looked up and saw the candy canes. Pudding was sure he was going to take them, but then one of the other reindeer in a nearby stall, Blitzen, neighed, and Rudolph turned away. Pudding sighed despairingly, but Santa looked like he'd just realised something and didn't like it.

'Do you have an idea about what's wrong with Rudolph?' Pudding asked hopefully.

'I'm afraid I might, Pudding dear,' Santa replied. He sounded sad, but then his voice turned strict. 'Vixen, Blitzen, Dasher, Dancer, Comet, Cupid, Donner, Prancer – get out here now,' Santa yelled.

Slowly, the eight reindeer trotted over, looking nervous. 'Now, I think I know what's going on,' said Santa, who was still speaking in that strict tone. 'I think you lot are up to your old tricks again!'

There was silence, until Donner walked over, head down, and neighed sadly.

'Thank you for your honesty, Donner, I'll remember that. Does anyone else wish to confess?' asked Santa.

Pudding watched in amazement as, one by one, the reindeer came up to Santa, like Donner had, and neighed their confession, until eventually, only Dasher had not confessed to Santa.

'Dasher? Is there anything you would like to add?' Santa questioned.

Dasher neighed angrily, as though insulted by the suggestion.

'That's funny,' Santa replied, 'because everyone else said that you were the ringleader!'

He turned around and clapped his hands together before speaking to the other reindeer. 'Okay, guys, you seven are very lucky to have fessed up, because Dasher here is next year's toilet cleaner!' Dasher's furry jaw dropped in surprise, but Santa continued speaking. 'Now, I want all of you to cheer Rudolph up and get the glow back in his nose!'

So, one by one, the reindeer lined up to crack a joke or pull a funny face, or even whistle the tune of 'Jingle Bells'! (This, surprisingly, was Dancer's talent. Pudding had assumed he would, well, dance.)

Then, to top it all off, the reindeer staged an apology musical, written and directed by Santa himself. By the end, Pudding was almost in tears with laughter and Rudolph's nose was glowing as brightly, if not more brightly, than before. He was ready to lead Santa's sleigh once more.

There was no time to waste, as the clock was ticking on Santa's deliveries. The Reindeer Care Team rushed to hook the reindeer on to the sleigh. Santa turned to Pudding and took a moment to acknowledge her clever thinking. 'Thank you, Pudding, for saving Christmas,' he said.

Pudding blushed. 'The only real hero is you, Santa! You're the one who found out what was wrong.'

'Ah, but you're the one who linked his mood to his nose,' replied Santa with a knowing smile, 'and as a special treat, I'd like to invite you to come with me on the sleigh tonight, what do you say?'

Pudding didn't have to think twice before answering, 'YES!'

And so, they set off delivering presents to all the children around the world, with Rudolph's glowing nose lighting the way, and Pudding felt the happiest she had in years.

Aimsigh na Difríochtaí 2

Aimsigh seacht ndifríocht idir an dá phictiúr.

Freagraí ar leathanach 78

Have you done Sudoku 1 on page 14? Once you've completed this second puzzle, you'll be on your way to becoming a sudoku master!

		8		4			7	
		1	7			3	4	6
			5					
	3	9						
	2		6		8		5	
						8	1	
					5			
3	1	4			6	7		
	8			3		6		

Answers on page 78

Read All About It:

2024'S BIG ANNIVERSARIES

Do you know what an anniversary is?

An anniversary is a date on which an event took place in the past. For example, if you moved into a new house on 4 March 2024, on 4 March 2025 it would the first anniversary of your house move.

The word anniversary comes from the Latin words 'annus', meaning year, and 'versus', which means turning.

Anniversaries are sometimes sad if they relate to tough events in our lives, but often they are happy occasions when we remember lovely things – for example, your birthday is the anniversary of your birth! Births, marriages and deaths are probably the mostly commonly marked anniversaries in our personal lives. Some people put notices in newspapers to acknowledge these occasions, and these pages are often called the 'Hatches, Matches and Dispatches'!

In the world of media, plenty of different anniversaries are often highlighted. This includes major moments in history, such as astronauts landing on the moon, discoveries of inventions and ends of wars; competition wins in the sporting calendar and anniversaries of much-loved albums, books and films. Countries sometimes celebrate the day they were founded.

Anniversaries can be a big deal when a particular amount of time has passed, for example, a 10th anniversary or 20th anniversary, or even a 50th or 100th anniversary!

Here are some notable anniversaries that occurred in 2024.

50 Years of Women Having Their Own Credit Cards

A credit card allows people to spend money from a lender and pay the lender back later. Payment cards were invented in the 1950s, and in 1958, Bank of America introduced the first modern credit card with a credit limit of $300. A person who was approved for the card could spend up to $300, without having that money themselves. Whenever they presented their card to pay a bill, for example, in a shop or restaurant, the bank would fund the payment. At the end of each month, the bank would send a bill to the credit card holder and require them to pay some of their balance. Banks charge a fee for credit, which is how they make money on credit cards. Despite credit cards being around since the 1950s, it was only in 1974 that it became possible for a woman in the USA to apply for her own credit card – the Equal Credit Opportunity Act was signed into law on 28 October that year. Before this, women were often discriminated against when applying for loans and often needed their husbands, fathers or brothers to co-sign before they could access credit. Though this is something that happened in another country, it is an important anniversary, as financial freedom allows people to improve their lives, by being able to afford things such as education or property. However, it is very important to be careful when using credit, as we must be sure we can pay it back. One of the first credit cards in Ireland was Ulster Bank's Access card, which was launched in 1972.

Other things that have been around for 50 years? The Rubik's cube and the barcode!

30 Years of *Riverdance*

Have you seen the Irish dancing stage act *Riverdance*? These days, there are many different companies of Irish dancers performing *Riverdance* shows all over the world, but the first *Riverdance* performance took place during the interval of the 1994 Eurovision Song Contest. The performance, including lead dancers Jean Butler and Michael Flatley, lasted just seven minutes but made such an impression on the 300-million-strong international audience watching Eurovision that night that it was soon clear that people wanted more. The music of *Riverdance*, composed by Bill Whelan and performed by Anúna and the RTÉ Concert Orchestra, was released as a single and topped the Irish charts for 18 weeks. In 1995, a full stage show was announced. A planned five-week run at the Point Theatre, Dublin, sold out in just three days. This was followed by a four-week run in London, and another six-week run in Dublin. In 1996, *Riverdance* was performed in New York for the first time, and had another extended run at the Apollo in London. By the end of 1996, *Riverdance* was so popular that a number of separate companies were set up to tour multiple cities at the same time. From 1997 onwards, *Riverdance* companies toured in such places as Australia and China. *Riverdance* has been seen live by more than 30 million people across 15,000 performances, 49 countries and six continents. In 2020, *Riverdance* toured a 25th anniversary show, and 2024 marks the 30th anniversary of the first performance of *Riverdance*. Though *Riverdance* is credited with reviving the popularity of Irish dance at home and abroad, interestingly, both of the original principal dancers, Jean Butler and Michael Flatley, are American.

25 Years of These Everyday Words

The terms blog, carbon footprint, dashcam, texting and vape were all recorded for the first time in 1999. 'Blog' has perhaps become less common nowadays, but the others are so frequently used, it's hard to believe they haven't been around for very long!

20 Years Since the Smoking Ban

As crazy as it might seem to you, before you were born, and up until 2004, people were allowed to smoke indoors in places such as pubs and restaurants. Those who remember going out at the time could tell you that as a result, many venues were smoky, unpleasant places and you could come home with the smell of smoke lingering on your clothes; not to mention, most importantly, that inhaling smoke wasn't very good for anyone's health. 20 years ago, when he was the Minister for Health, Micheál Martin introduced the smoking ban, giving everyone clean air in indoor venues. Worth celebrating!

Other things that are 20 years old? Facebook and Gmail!

10 Years of the Wild Atlantic Way

Ireland has always been popular with tourists, but the Wild Atlantic Way tourism trail on the west coast truly shows off the power of good marketing. The Wild Atlantic Way is the name given to a 2,600 km driving route that stretches from Donegal down to Cork and allows tourists to visit such sights as the Cliffs of Moher, the Dingle Peninsula and the Old Head of Kinsale, as well as experiencing Irish culture, heritage and food in towns and villages across nine counties. All in all, there are more than 1,000 attractions and 2,500 activities along the full drive. The route was officially launched by the Minister for Tourism of the time, Michael Ring TD, in 2014, making this year the 10th anniversary of the Wild Atlantic Way. Analysis of its impact shows that it has attracted millions of visitors from around the world, with two million more people per year visiting now than in 2013. It has boosted tourism in the local economies along the route, with tourism in the west now estimated to be worth €3 billion per year, and has created 35,000 jobs and helped to preserve the heritage of the west coast of Ireland. In fact, 51% of all tourist revenue in Ireland is generated on the west coast. Not bad for an idea that had an investment of €10 million back in 2014 ... quite a lot of money, but not very much compared with the results!

What anniversaries are coming in 2025?

2025 will mark:

- The 75th anniversary of the delicious German food, currywurst!
- The 70th anniversary of Rosa Parks' arrest for refusing to give up her seat on a bus, a well-known event in US civil rights history.
- The 25th anniversary of Sony's PlayStation 2 games console.
- The 25th anniversary of the first residential crew going to live on the International Space Station, which has been continuously occupied since.
- The 20th anniversary of YouTube.
- The 15th anniversary of the Apple iPad and Instagram.
- The 10th anniversary of the global climate change pact at the COP 21 summit in Paris, the first time all countries committed to reducing carbon emissions in response to climate change.

Duine Cáiliúil:

Olivia Rodrigo

Rugadh Olivia Rodrigo ar an 20 Feabhra 2003 i gCalifornia sna Stáit Aontaithe. Is páiste aonair í. Thosaigh sí ag déanamh ceachtanna canadh ag aois a 5, ansin thosaigh sí ceachtanna pianó ag aois a 9 agus bhí sí ag seinm an ghiotair ag aois a 12.

Is cantóir agus aisteoir í agus tá cáil uirthi as ucht a ceol iontach agus a rólanna éagsúla ar an teilifís. Tháinig clú agus cáil uirthi ar dtús nuair a bhí sí ar an seó *Bizaardvark* ar an Disney Channel agus níos déanaí ar an seó *High School Musical: The Musical: The Series* ar Disney+.

I mí Eanáir 2021, d'eisigh sí a céad amhrán 'drivers license'. Bhí an-tóir ar an amhrán agus bhí grá ag daoine ar fud an domhain dó mar gheall ar na liricí croíúla. D'eisigh sí a céad albam *SOUR* i mí Bealtaine 2021. Tá amhráin cáiliúla eile ar nós 'déjà vu' agus 'good 4 u' ar an albam sin.

Tá cáil ar cheol Olivia toisc go bhfuil sé macánta agus bunaithe ar mhothúcháin agus a bheith ag fás aníos. Déanann a lán daoine óga nascadh le hamhráin de chuid Olivia ar na fáthanna seo. Taobh amuigh de cheol iontach a dhéanamh, bíonn Olivia ag labhairt amach faoi rudaí tábhachtacha ar nós meabhairshláinte agus cearta na mban, ag mealladh daoine óga le bheith láidir agus muiníneach.

Is réalta í Olivia Rodrigo, ní hamháin toisc an bua sa cheol agus san aisteoireacht atá aici, ach toisc go n-úsáideann sí a guth chun tionchar dearfach a bheith aici ar an domhan.

FIRICÍ FÁNACHA faoi Olivia Rodrigo

- Bhí a céad singil 'drivers license' ar bharr na cairteacha (Billboard Hot 100) ar feadh ocht seachtaine i ndiaidh a chéile.
- Bhí an-tionchar ag Taylor Swift, Lorde agus Alanis Morissette uirthi. Tá Taylor Swift tar éis a cuid scríbhneoireachta a mholadh.
- Bhuaigh Olivia trí dhuais Grammy i 2022: Ceoltóir nua is fearr, Albam pop gutha is fearr don albam *SOUR* agus cur i láthair aonair pop is fearr don singil 'drivers license'.
- Tá cáil uirthi as ucht a liricí macánta, goilliúnacha; déanann Olivia chomhscríbhneoireacht ar a cuid ceoil.
- Labhraíonn sí amach faoi athrú aeráide agus úsáideann sí a cuid cáile chun inbhuanaitheacht a chur chun cinn.
- Éireannaigh, Gearmánaigh agus Filipínigh a bhí ina sinisir.

Spot the Difference 3

Can you find the ten small differences between these two winter scenes?

Answers on page 78

Festival Christmas Writing Competition Runner-up:

The Magic of Winter Wonderland

by Ellie Ó Mórdha, Scoil Áine, Raheny, Dublin 5

Snowflakes were gently falling from the yellowish grey clouds. I woke in the cold white snow to see a gorgeous young wolf cub staring up at me, his head cocked questioningly to one side. I gasped out loud and frantically scrambled backwards. He whimpered and lay down in the snow, his snubby nose tucked in his paws, gazing at me shyly. I realised he was friendly, and cautiously reached out my shaking fingers for him to sniff. I noticed his soft-grey colour and cute, fluffy belly. The cub shot out a bright-red tongue and I flinched, but he started to lick my freezing hand.

'Hello, little guy,' I whispered softly to him, gazing into his big, green eyes. All at once, it hit me why I was here. I had gone wandering and got lost, and my parents were away hunting for food. I sighed sadly and looked in the bag I had brought along with me. I pulled out a tin opener, bread and some tinned tuna. The cub hungrily licked his small, black nose.

'I wonder what to call you,' I muttered as I spread tuna on a slice of bread with a pocketknife and offered it to the cub. 'Streaky, maybe?' The cub looked up from his food and gave a little snort of disgust. 'Okay, okay, maybe not!' I laughed. 'Smudge, perhaps?'

'Owww, oww, oww,' howled the cub.

'Okay, okay. Smudge it is' I chuckled. 'Right, let's get on with our trip then.'

Smudge started to claw at my long scarf and got caught, so I gently unhooked his little claws, and we went on our way. We walked over the slopes. I carried Smudge over the steep hills of ice. We were not aiming for a particular direction. We just had to keep on going and going to keep warm.

Suddenly, I heard a bird crying. I trudged as quickly as I could through the deep snow. It was a baby seagull. I took off my gloves and stuffed them in my pocket. I scooped up the little fledgling. His body was frozen and tiny. His thin, baby feathers were damp, and bits of frost stuck to them. He was shivering violently and that was when I noticed a small cut on his right wing, with little stains of dried blood dotted around it. I rummaged in my bag and found a small bottle of healing ointment and gently smeared the yellow oil on the cut.

I took the remains of the tuna and offered it to the bird. He pecked up the scraps hungrily and, when he was finished, I carefully tucked him in the fluffy pocket of my thick coat.

'Come on, Smudge,' I said to the quiet, watching cub, 'let's go on our way.' I started to move, and Smudge followed. I peeped in my pocket to check on the gull and I saw him nestled down, blinking up at me sleepily.

As I walked on, I wondered if I would be home in time for Christmas. According to my calculations, it was Christmas Eve! I shook my head sternly and said to myself: *Ella, no point in sulking! It won't get you anywhere!* So, I pushed it to the back of my mind.

The journey was going well until Smudge pranced playfully onto some thin, slippery ice and a long, scary crack appeared, before breaking off the piece of ice he was standing on.

'Smudge!' I screamed in panic, trying desperately to think of an idea to save the little wolf. My mind went completely blank. My eyes welled up with tears and I cried in frustration. In a flash, I had an idea. My scarf! I unwound it quickly, remembering how Smudge had been playing with it. I hurled one end towards Smudge, and it miraculously landed where he was standing.

'Get it, boy! Get it!' I coaxed encouragingly to Smudge and eventually he grabbed it with his strong jaws. I puffed until my face turned red and, with effort, hauled him along the ice. When he was near, I reached out and cuddled him close, breathing in his scent and kissing the tufty fur on his small head. I bundled him in my scarf to keep him safe and cautiously leaned beside a break in the ice and caught a big, silver fish for him to eat.

We went on walking and all of a sudden, Smudge tore away! I raced after him, panting hard. I gasped, for there right in front of us, nuzzling Smudge, was a beautiful white wolf. She had massive, fluffy paws, a strong tail and a button-shaped, black nose just like her son's. Her big, gorgeous eyes stared at me. She whined quietly and I found myself brave enough to run a hand over her smooth, glossy coat. The majestic wolf licked me briefly, barked to Smudge and together they bounded off. I was sad to see them go.

Then, I heard voices calling. It was my parents! I looked around, saw them standing close by, and ran over and leapt into their arms. I showed them the seagull and they smiled and hugged me tightly.

'We missed you so much, Ella,' they said. I thought about Smudge and his mum. I grinned and took my parents' hands. I was happy, for I was going home.

Recipe: Fancy Ice!

This is a very simple, but very delicious way to add some extra fanciness to your Christmas celebrations. It's also quite a good way to add some fruit to your day at a time when you might be having lots of fun foods!

Great combos:

- Cranberry juice ice cubes with frozen raspberries in sparkling water
- Plain water ice cubes with frozen blueberries in lemonade
- Plain water ice cubes with frozen mint and strawberry pieces in still or sparkling water
- Coconut milk ice cubes with iced tea
- Lemon juice ice cubes with frozen orange pieces in sparkling water

Equipment:

- Ice cube tray
- Chopping board and knife

What to do:

1. Choose your liquid. It could be water, or you might like to try juices such as lemon, lime or orange, or even coconut milk.
2. Choose your add-ins. Options include mint leaves, blueberries, raspberries and strawberry slices.
3. Ensure your add-ins are washed, if needed. Chop if required, and place some in each section of the ice cube tray.
4. Pour in liquid right to the top.
5. Place in the freezer until solid.
6. Choose a drink and pop in some fancy ice. Enjoy!

Tip!

Your ice cubes will store in the freezer for up to six months.

JUST HAVING A LAUGH!

Where do bad rainbows go?
Prism. It's a light sentence that gives them some time to reflect!

Did I tell you that I'm going to the world polishing championships? It's my time to shine!

What did the 0 say to the 8?
Nice belt!

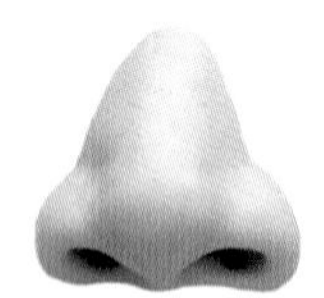

What did the right eye say to the left eye?
Just between the two of us, something smells!

How do you fit more pigs on a small farm?
Build a styscraper.

Did you hear about the man who had his left side removed? He's alright now!

What do you call a mackerel in a bow tie?
So-fish-ticated.

I saw an ad in the window of an electronics shop: TV for sale, €1, volume stuck on loud. I thought to myself, I can't turn that down!

How does a snowman lose weight?
He waits for warmer weather.

What breed of dogs make good magicians?
Labracadabradors!

A gingerbread man went to the doctor because his leg cracked off. The doctor said, have you tried icing it?

How does the moon cut his hair?
Eclipse it.

Sudoku 3

Have you done Sudoku 1 and Sudoku 2 on pages 14 and 23? Try this third puzzle as one last practice before the big sudoku star challenge on page 55.

		3		4	7			1
			8	2			3	
6	7		3			2		
				6				8
	2	5				4	7	
8				5				
		1			2		6	4
	4			7	8			
9			4	1		8		

Answers on page 78

Christmas Crafts:
Make Your Own Gonk

Have you noticed how popular gonk decorations have become at Christmastime? These cute little dolls with their big hats, long beards and snub noses seem to be everywhere, and the great news is, if you would like to have one or even give one as a thoughtful gift, they are quite simple to make!

You will need:

- A big, long sock
- A pint glass
- Bag of uncooked rice
- Elastic band or hair tie
- Make-up brush and powder
- A scrap of fabric in a festive colour such as green or red, or an old baby or doll's hat, or another sock!
- Needle and thread
- Cotton wool
- Glue
- Ball of white, cream or grey wool
- Scissors

Be safe!
Ask an adult for help with cutting and stitching.

What to do:

1. Fill a pint glass to the top with uncooked rice.
2. To make the gonk's body, cut the large sock underneath the heel, fill it with rice and then tie the top, loosely for the moment. Keep the rest of the sock.
3. Take the sock of rice and pinch out a ball of rice at the front between your finger and thumb. Place an elastic band or thin hair tie around it to make the gonk's nose. If you wish, use a make-up brush and some powder to dust the nose to a skin colour. Now, tie the top of the sock tightly shut.

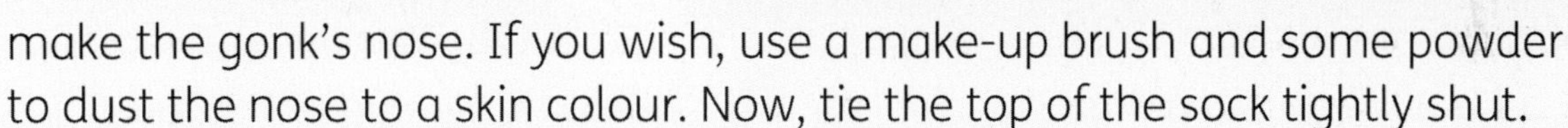

4. There are a number of ways to make the gonk's hat:
   - Take the scrap of green or red fabric and cut it into a triangle – the larger the triangle, the larger the hat. Using your needle and thread, overlap and stitch two sides together to make a gonk hat. Stuff it with some cotton wool, then glue the hat to the top of the gonk's body.
   - Use the other half of the sock (or another sock, if you would like to vary the patterns), and place it on the gonk's head.
   - Use an old baby's or doll's hat if you happen to have one lying around.
5. To make the gonk's beard, wind 10–20 lengths of wool (depending on the size of your gonk) around your hand, then slide them off. Take a separate piece of wool just a few centimetres long, and tie this tightly around the centre of your wound wool. It should look like a bow tie. Using a scissors, chop open each end of the bow tie. It will now look like a shaggy beard! Use some glue to stick it on just below the gonk's nose.

   Et voila, your very own DIY gonk!

Tip!

If you plan to stitch your gonk hat and have not learned to stitch before, try watching an online tutorial by searching for hand sewing videos on YouTube.
Ask an adult for help with stitching and using scissors.

Best Posts of 2024

Michael Fry
@BigDirtyFry

I had to get off my bus earlier because the driver told us he realised he'd been driving round with the wrong number on the front and all the wrong people got on. I wasn't even mad. He's almost definitely just back after a long holiday.

00:32 · 11/01/2024 From Earth · **60K** Views

18 Reposts **4** Quotes **832** Likes **8** Bookmarks

This bus driver shows how hard it is to get back to regular life in January!

J. Courtney Sullivan
@jcourtsull
Follow

Got flagged by airport security because my son had a Magic 8 Ball in his backpack. Two TSA agents debated whether it was ok. My husband said, "If only we had a simple way to answer a yes or no question..." Crickets.

02:22 · 20/04/2024 From Earth · **2.7M** Views

5.4K Reposts **199** Quotes

This dad did not get enough credit for that line!

chi
@ChiThukral

i think leap day should be a internationally observed holiday - you're telling me we get an extra day every FOUR years and we have to work?? that doesn't sit right w me

Last edited 11:08 AM · 2/27/24 From Earth · **1.8M** Views

8.8K Reposts **331** Quotes

This is definitely an opinion we can get behind.

Liz Charboneau
@lizchar

Air and Space Museum should have a plane emergency slide you can go down just to get to experience it

6:33 PM · 4/9/24 · **316K** Views

600 Reposts **37** Quotes **15K** Likes **150** Bookmarks

It would be a bit of a long haul for us to visit the Air and Space Museum in Washington, DC, but hey, Dublin Airport, this would be a great way to pass some time in the baggage claim area!

John Moe
@johnmoe

Because I never explained otherwise, my son spent a good stretch of time in his childhood thinking that a vice principal at a school was there in case the principal was assassinated.

1:52 PM · 4/9/24 From Earth · **670K** Views

1.4K Reposts **108** Quotes

Guys, this is not why you have a vice principal!

Amanda
@Pandamoanimum

Just met 4 dachshunds in the park called Gary, Steve, Kevin and Dave, and my day improved by approximately 659%

8:05 AM · 4/12/24 From Earth · **768K** Views

786 Reposts **56** Quotes **26K** Likes **431** Bookmarks

We need to know where this park is immediately and we'll be dachshund right over there – animals with human names are the best.

Kale Williams
@sfkale

a truck carrying 100k chinook salmon smolts (yay!) crashed in eastern oregon and flipped over (oh no!) but did so right above a creek (yay!) and a bunch died (oh no!) but more than 75k of them were inadvertently released and will likely return there to spawn as adults (yay!)

5:52 PM · 4/2/24 From Earth · **392K** Views

946 Reposts **117** Quotes **12K** Likes **444** Bookmarks

This is ... 75% good news?

Irish Literary Times
@IrishLitTimes

Don't know who to credit for this one

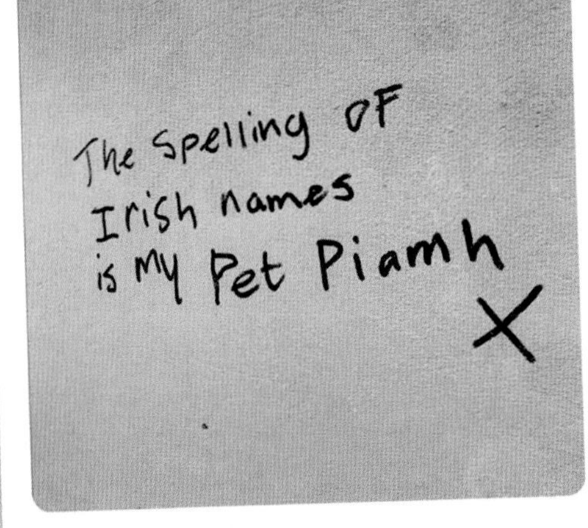

4:26 PM · 2/25/24 · **451K** Views

892 Reposts **74** Quotes **10K** Likes **420** Bookmarks

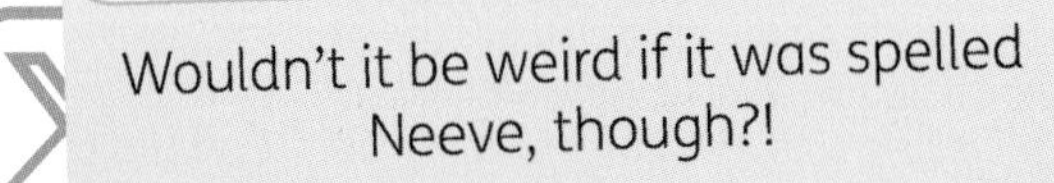

Wouldn't it be weird if it was spelled Neeve, though?!

Karen Knight
@KarenKn12866337

This tree looks like it's sneaking out of the woods. 😁

3:58 AM · 2/18/24 From Earth · **4.8M** Views

It really does!

Thanos.
@Slim_Thanos

I was pulled over by a Police Officer . He looked at my license and said "you're supposed to be wearing glasses". I said I have contacts. He said he didn't care who I know

4:46 AM · 2/26/24 From Earth · **10M** Views

18K Reposts **3.1K** Quotes

Hah!

Festival Christmas Writing Competition Runner-up:

Santa's Magic Hat

by Elise Di Lucia, St Brigid's Girls National School, Dublin

Once upon a time, there were two girls, Tinsel and Bauble. These lovely girls were Santa's daughters, though they were not human, as Santa's magic made it dangerous for him to have children, but life-sized toys with human hearts. They felt and thought just like normal children, but they had special perks, like how amazing Bauble was at inventing or how spectacular Tinsel was at magic.

One night, Bauble and Tinsel were getting ready for bed, when they saw that the door to Santa's room was wide open. His wardrobe was spilling out and sitting on top of the pile of clothes was his magical hat.

'I'll get it before you do!' giggled Tinsel, running into the cosy room and grabbing the hat.

'Tinsel, we're not supposed to be in here,' exclaimed Bauble, 'if we lose that hat, Santa won't be able to deliver the toys for the little children!' Bauble started to walk into the room and grab for the hat, but she missed as Tinsel hopped aside.

'No, no, no, Bauble! I'm gonna ...' but before Tinsel could finish, a gust of wind came in from the open window and took the hat off her head.

'Oh no, Tinsel, for elves' sake! Couldn't you just listen? How shall we find it now?'

Bauble fretted, running to the window to try and grab for the hat, but it had floated over the border of Santa's village now and was far from Bauble's reach, even with her special abilities.

'Oh, I'm sorry ...' sighed Tinsel.

'Let's go, maybe we can catch it if we fly with reindeer!' Bauble smiled, running down the stairs, her clever brain whirring at a million miles per hour, and Tinsel at her heels.

Once they got to the stables, Bauble jumped on Dancer and said, 'Come on, Tinsel! Jump on Prancer and say the spell you learned the other day!'

'Alright!' little Tinsel said, happy to be of use. She clicked her fingers and spun a ball of magic in her palms. 'Bibbity, bobbity, boo,' giggled Tinsel, casting the spell on the reindeer as she hopped onto Prancer.

'On, Dancer!' cried Bauble, followed by an, 'On, Prancer!' from Tinsel. But the reindeer did not fly.

An older reindeer piped up from a nearby stall, 'For goodness sake! Reindeer can't fly unless it's Christmas Eve! Everyone knows that! I thought at least Santa's children would!'

'Oh no! How will we find the hat now?' frowned Tinsel, realising that what the old reindeer said was true.

Bauble thought for a moment and then asked, 'How about Salt and Pepper?' pointing at the two donkeys in the corner.

'Yes! I'll try the magic spell on them!' Tinsel laughed, and with another quick flick of her wrist, and a quick 'Bibbity, bobbity, boo!' the two girls and their donkeys rose into the air.

'Let's go! Only twelve hours until the morning of Christmas Eve!' exclaimed Bauble, and they rode off into the night.

The donkeys were unsteady, and flew clumsily over mountain tops and sugar drops, but after what seemed like hours, Tinsel and Bauble saw the hat. They flew down to try and catch it, but it was stuck in a magic wind. No matter how hard they tried, they could not grab it before it was whisked away.

'Bauble, I don't think this is a normal wind ...' Tinsel shouted to her sister over the noise of the breeze, 'I think this is one of Jack Frost's winds!'

'Oh no! We won't be able to get it until Jack Frost lets us, which could be never!' Bauble fretted, still trying to grab a hold of the hat.

'Perhaps we could steal it back!' Tinsel laughed.

'Yes! That's perfect! C'mon, let's try to get to Jack Frost before the hat does,' said Bauble.

And so, the girls were off, flying far and wide until they reached the cold wintery cave that was home to Jack Frost. Dismounting the donkeys, they snuck inside and hid behind a boulder.

'My new hat shall arrive any moment!' A voice came, as sharp as an icicle and as cold as snow. Jack Frost stepped into the girls' view and did a little dance. He still didn't see the girls and said to himself, 'Silly children, Silly Santa. I am the brains. I shall finally show Santa that my smarts and my magic will always pass out him and his daughters.'

There was a momentary silence, before Tinsel stood up. 'You evil, no-good MONSTER! No wonder nobody loves you!' she shouted, and pulled up a ball of magic in her hands. It was bright red, the colour of love, but also the colour of danger and anger.

Tinsel is going to overuse her powers, thought Bauble, *I need a way to stop her, and contain Jack Frost ...*

Suddenly, Bauble had an idea. She snuck around the other side of the boulder and cast out a dagger. It stuck in the ice on the ceiling, cutting a slab free, and the ice fell at such an angle that it separated Tinsel and Jack Frost.

Just then, the hat arrived, and Bauble grabbed it. Then, she reached out to hook an arm around Tinsel's small body and dragged her sister from where she stood. Bauble ran like the wind down to where the donkeys were resting. She put Tinsel on Salt and jumped on Pepper herself. Little Tinsel muttered the spell again for the donkeys to fly and soon they were up in the sky, Santa's hat in Bauble's hand and Jack Frost's angry screams following them.

When they got home, they put the hat back where it belonged and made sure to close the windows.

'You know, Bauble, that was actually lots of fun!' admitted Tinsel.

'I know, Tinsel, I enjoyed it too,' said Bauble.

The girls giggled and vowed to never go on another adventure without each other.

And, just to let you boys and girls know, Santa had the most successful Christmas ever that year, as the story spread around the world of how Santa's daughters had saved Christmas. It raised the Christmas spirit by 50%, bringing the spirit to 99.99999%.

Can you guess who the other .00001% is?

That's right. It's Jack Frost.

Celebrity Profile

Daniel Wiffen

Born: 14 July 2001
From: Magheralin, Co. Armagh
Star sign: Cancer

Irish swimmer Daniel Wiffen was born in England, but moved with his family to Magheralin, Co. Armagh, in Northern Ireland when he was two. Wiffen has dual citizenship, which means he is a citizen of both Ireland and Britain. This means that he can represent either country in swimming competitions. He represents Ireland at the Olympic Games, and the World and European championships, but swims for Northern Ireland in the Commonwealth Games.

Daniel and his twin brother Nathan started swimming at three months old. Both began swimming in local competitions when they joined Lurgan Swimming Club at age six. Later, they qualified for the Ulster squad under coach Stan Sheppard at Lisburn City Swimming Club. Nathan specialised in backstroke while Daniel preferred freestyle.

In 2014, aged 13, Daniel qualified for the Irish squad, and working with local coaches Richard Gheel and later Martin J. McGann, began to climb through the swimming rankings and set Irish records.

During Covid lockdowns, the Wiffen brothers stayed swimming, using a paddling pool with a tether, and catching up with their coach via video calls.

Wiffen is a student at Loughborough University, studying Computer Science.

When Wiffen represented Ireland at the 2024 World Championships, he set a freestyle short-course world record in the 800 m race with a time of 7 minutes and 20.46 seconds. He is the first Irish male swimmer to become a world champion. His parents, Rachel and Jonathan, were only there to see the record-setting moment as he bought them flights as a last-minute Christmas gift! Wiffen had previously become the first Irishman to hold a European swimming record when he broke the 800 m freestyle record in 2022. He also broke a European long-course record at the 2023 World Aquatics Championships.

Wiffen's Wins

- 2024 Olympic Games Paris 800 m freestyle Gold
- 2024 Olympic Games Paris 1500 m freestyle Bronze
- 2024 World Championships Doha 800 m freestyle Gold
- 2024 World Championships Doha 1500 m freestyle Gold
- 2023 European Championships Otopeni 400 m freestyle Gold
- 2023 European Championships Otopeni 800 m freestyle Gold
- 2023 European Championships Otopeni 1500 m freestyle Gold
- 2023 U-23 European Championships Dublin 400 m freestyle Silver
- 2023 U-23 European Championships Dublin 800 m freestyle Silver
- 2023 U-23 European Championships Dublin 1500 m freestyle Gold
- 2022 Commonwealth Games Birmingham 1500 m freestyle Silver

Interesting Facts

- ✓ As well as having a twin, Wiffen has two older siblings, Beth and Ben, and the family have a pet tortoise called Flash.
- ✓ The Wiffen siblings appeared in an episode of *Game of Thrones*.

Wiffen in Quotes

- 'It's massive, it's the biggest medal I've ever got and it's very heavy. It's definitely a World Championships medal. You can tell that by the size of it. It's pretty cool. I think I was holding it for about an hour because so many people wanted photos with me with it. It took me a while to take it off. I had it around my neck for a long time because I was just taking in the moment. It's just amazing to say that I am world champion.'

Amazing Words

Here at *Festival* HQ, we love adding new words to our vocabulary.
Here is an A–Z of some of the best ones we've heard this year.

Abecedarian

Did you know that you were once an abecedarian? Sounds fancy, doesn't it? But this impressive word, coming from the Latin *abecedarius*, which means 'alphabetical', simply refers to someone who is learning the alphabet.

Balderdash

Balderdash means nonsense, but it's a lot more fun to say!

Camelry

You may know that soldiers or troops on horseback are called the cavalry, but did you know that troops on camels are called the camelry?

Driblet

A very small part of something, such as a drop of liquid.

Epistaxis

You've almost certainly experienced this, even if you don't know what it is. Epistaxis is a term for a nosebleed. If it was a very minor nosebleed, would we call it a driblet?

Fie!

Rhyming with 'eye', this is a word to use when you want to show that you are disgusted.

Gregarious

A gregarious person is someone who likes to be with other people.

Hyperbole

Hyperbole is exaggeration. Be careful saying this one out loud as it might look like the last part is pronounced 'bowl', but it's actually more like 'buh-lee'.

Incorrigible

Misbehaving children are sometimes described as incorrigible because they are hard to manage and do not wish to change. Depending on your point of view, calling someone incorrigible might be seen as positive or negative!

Jovial

A jovial person is known for how good-natured they are. What a delight!

Kindred

Things that are kindred are alike; they have similar natures or similar characteristics. They can also, literally, be related, i.e. of the same kin. Have you ever been described as kindred spirits with someone?

Laudable

Something or someone that is laudable deserves praise.

Malady

A malady is a disease or condition. Next time you're ill, you might call it a malady. If your sickness is very mild and you call it a malady, though, you might be accused of hyperbole!

Nimble

Nimble refers to quick, light, clever movements. They can be physical or mental, for example, you might have 'nimble fingers' if you're good at piano, but you could also say someone has a 'nimble wit' if they are very good at quick-witted responses!

Outlandish

Something is outlandish if it's bizarre, strange or unusual. For example, having spaghetti with chocolate sauce for dinner may be delicious, but it's certainly outlandish!

Persnickety

Someone who is persnickety is very fussy about small details.

Quarrel

Quarrel means an argument or dispute. If you quarrel with your parents over the tidiness of your room, it might be because you find them persnickety about how you keep your things ... or maybe you are outlandishly messy!

Rookie

A rookie is someone who is new to a situation. The exact meaning refers to new sports recruits in their first year playing for a team, but over time people have used the word rookie to mean 'newbie' more generally!

Serene

A serene person or place is calm, and untroubled by conditions around them!

Transgression

A transgression is the breaking of a limit or rule. For example, if your family rule is that you must be home by 8 p.m., and you do not arrive back until 8.30 p.m., that would be a transgression.

Usurp

If you usurp something, you take it without having the right to. It usually refers to positions more than things. For example, in history, you might read about a person usurping a throne when they were not the crowned king or queen, or the next in line.

Vamoose

To vamoose is to leave quickly. (Should a speedy moose be called a vamoose? We think so!)

Wamble

To wamble is to move unsteadily or feel sick.

Xanthic

Something that is xanthic has a yellowy colour.

Yardstick

The exact measure of a yardstick is three feet, but the term is used to mean any measure of quality or standard. For example, 'It was a great car, by any yardstick.'

Zeal

To be zealous or full of zeal is to be very interested and eager.

Sumoji!

Can you work out the value of each emoji to solve the sums below?

Sumoji 1

🍪🍪🍪🍪🍪🍪 + 🍪🍪 + 🍪 = 45

🍪🍪🍪🍪🍪🍪 + ⭐⭐⭐⭐ = 38

🎅🎅 + ⭐⭐⭐⭐⭐⭐⭐ + 🍪 = 25

🎅 + ⭐⭐⭐⭐⭐⭐ + 🍪🍪 = ?

Sumoji 2

❄❄❄❄❄ + ❄❄❄❄ – ❄ = 32

🦌🦌 + 🦌🦌🦌 + 🦌🦌🦌🦌🦌 = 60

🦌 + ❄ + 🛷🛷🛷🛷🛷🛷🛷🛷 = 18

🦌 + ❄ + 🛷 = ?

Sumoji 3

🔴🔴🔴🔴🔴🔴 + 🔴🔴🔴 – 🔴 = 56

🔴🔴🔴 – 🎀 = 13

🔴 + 🎀 – ⛄ = 6

🔴🔴 + 🎀🎀 + ⛄⛄ = ?

Sumoji 4

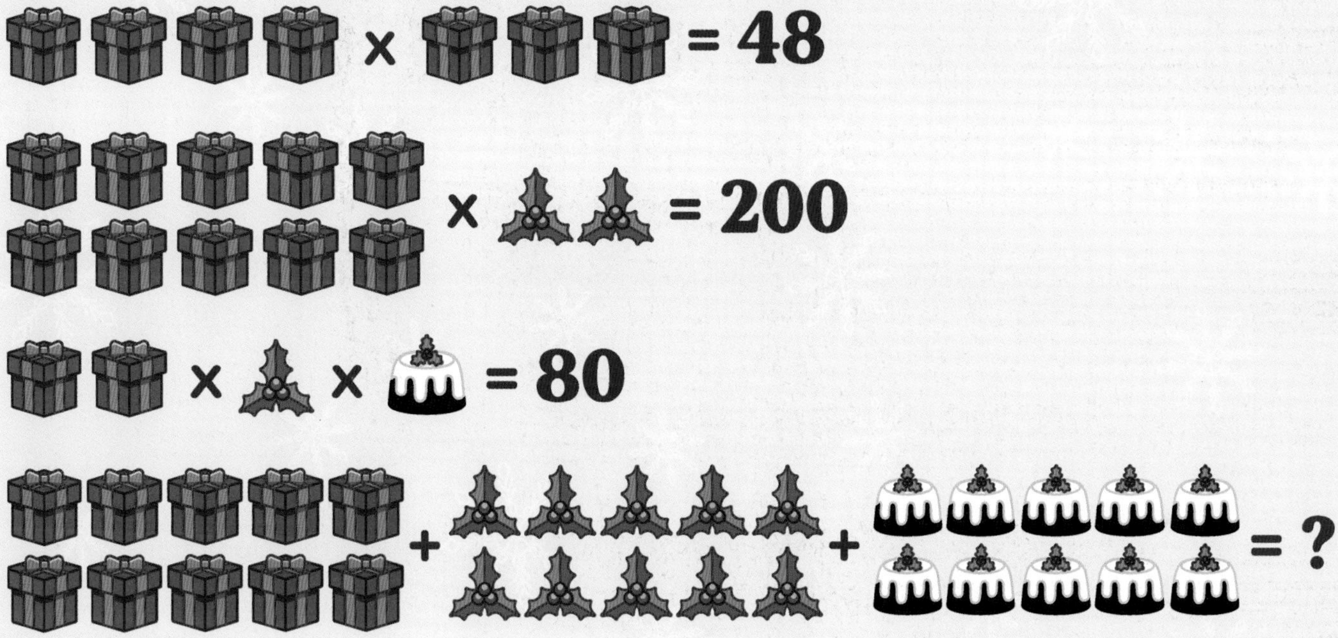

× = 48

× = 200

× × = 80

+ + = ?

Sumoji 5

+ = 37

× × = 189

+ + = ?

Sumoji 6

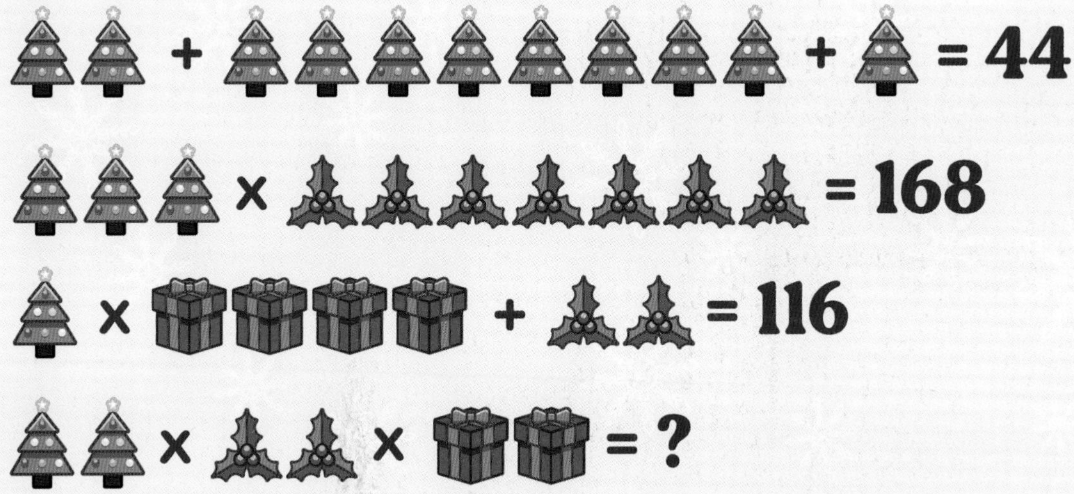

+ + = 44

× = 168

× + = 116

× × = ?

Answers on page 78

CLUEDLE!

Have you ever played the online word game Wordle? Then you might like to try *Festival*'s similar word game – Cluedle!

- ✓ In each word puzzle below there is a grid with six rows.
- ✓ The first five rows can be completed by inserting the correct word for the given clue – it may help to know that each answer can only be a five-letter word!
- ✓ In the sixth row there is no clue – you must work out the word using information you have gained from the first five words in the grid.
- ✓ You will see that each of the first five rows has some squares shaded in yellow and some in green. Yellow shading means that the letter you have filled in by answering the clue is a letter that appears in the sixth row, but not in the column shown. Green shading means the letter you have filled in by answering the clue is a letter that appears in the sixth row, in the same column.
- ✓ Each time you reveal a letter shaded in green, you should fill it into the correct place in the sixth row.
- ✓ Each time you reveal a letter shaded in yellow, you should make note of it.
- ✓ When you have filled in all of the green letters you have discovered, figure out the final word by working out where the yellow letters belong. Do this by excluding the spaces where they cannot go – for example, because there is already a green letter filled in, or because the letter has appeared in that column in yellow.
- ✓ Remember: the final word will only contain the letters you have discovered in green and yellow – no other letters will be part of the word.

When we say 'row', we mean a line going left to right. When we say 'column', we mean a line going top to bottom.

PUZZLE 1

1. The number of legs a spider has
2. Evaporated water
3. A light, covered canoe with an opening for a person
4. A dance where you bend backwards to pass under a low bar
5. A type of fungus that can be used to make bread!
6. ?

PUZZLE 2

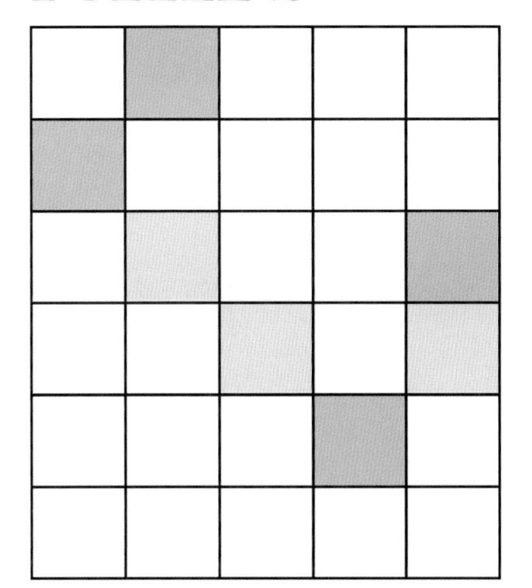

1. An automatic action that is hard to give up
2. The liquid version of a fruit
3. Type of cutlery: versions include tea, soup and dessert
4. Skin covering the top of the head
5. A fun food, or to provide care
6. ?

PUZZLE 3

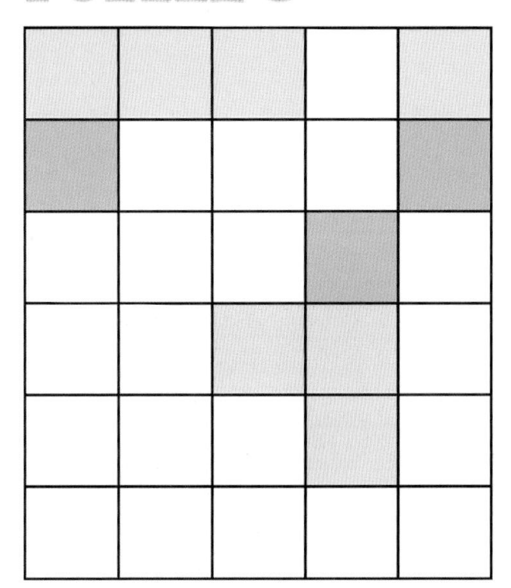

1. A bird of prey, or a golf score
2. Person aged 18 or over
3. Cannot see
4. A period of time between 28 and 31 days, depending on the calendar
5. Picture taken with a camera
6. ?

PUZZLE 4

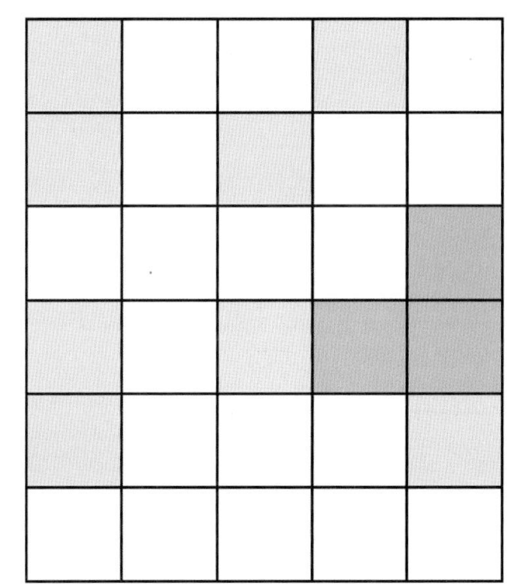

1. State in the USA known as the Lone Star
2. Vehicle that moves on a track, or to practise a skill
3. To turn red, for example, in the cheeks
4. A type of bus, or a person who provides training
5. A weapon shot from a bow
6. ?

Answers on page 78

CLUEDLE AS GAEILGE!

Bain triail as Cluedle as Gaeilge – leagan *Festival* den chluiche Wordle.

- ✓ Tá sé sraith i ngach puzal.
- ✓ Líon isteach an chéad cúig sraith ag baint úsáide as na leideanna – tá cúig litir i ngach freagra!
- ✓ Níl aon leid do shraith a sé – caithfidh tú an focal a oibriú amach ag baint úsáide as an eolas a d'aimsigh tú sa chéad cúig focal.
- ✓ Tá roinnt boscaí ann atá glas nó buí. Ciallaíonn buí go bhfuil an litir ceart ach sa cholún mícheart. Ciallaíonn glas go bhfuil an litir ceart sa cholún ceart.
- ✓ Gach uair go bhfaigheann tú litir glas, ba chóir duit é a líonadh isteach san áit cheart sa séú sraith.
- ✓ Nuair atá na litreacha glasa go léir aimsithe agat, oibrigh amach an focal sa séú sraith tré úsáid a bhaint as na litreacha buí atá fágtha agat.
- ✓ Cuimhnigh: ní bheidh ach nach litreacha glasa agus buí sa séú focal – ní bheidh aon litreacha nua mar chuid den fhocal.

Nuair a deirtear 'sraith', táimid ag labhairt faoi líne ag dul ó chlé go deas. Nuair a deirtear 'colún', táimid ag labhairt faoi líne ag dul ó bharr go bun.

PUZAL 1

1. Cúig móide cúig cothrom le _______________.
2. Baineann _______________ le plandaí agus ainmhithe.
3. Bhuaigh mé _______________ sa chomórtas scríbhneoireachta.
4. Cén saghas _______________ atá agat? Tá madra agam.
5. Bíonn breithimh agus dlíodóirí ag obair san áit seo.
6. ?

PUZAL 2

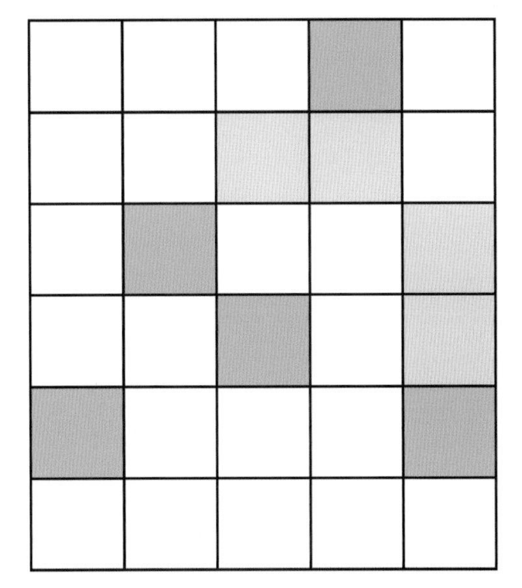

1. Bhí Daidí Béar, ______________ Béar agus Babaí Béar amuigh ag siúl.
2. Tá tart orm, an bhfuil cead agam ______________ a fháil?
3. Mhair an ______________ Mór ó 1845 go 1852.
4. Tríocha méadaithe fá thrí cothrom le ______________.
5. Focal eile ar veidhlín.
6. ?

PUZAL 3

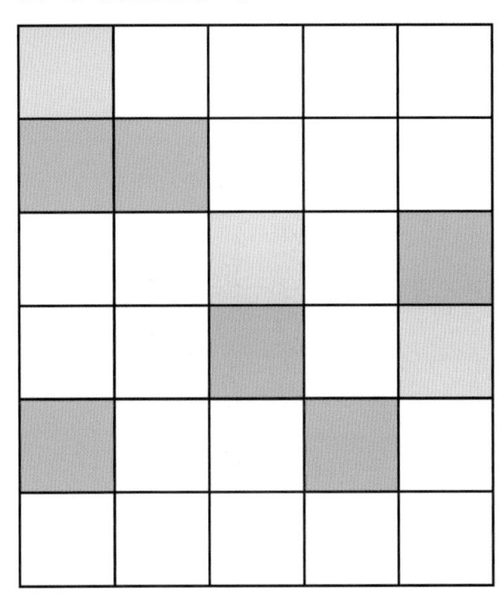

1. Scríobh mé ______________ chuig mo thuismitheoirí nuair a bhí mé sa ghaeltacht.
2. Is ______________ mhór í carraig.
3. Bhí cáca ______________ agam do mo bhreithlá.
4. Sheinn Ringo Starr na ______________ í leis an mbanna ceoil the Beatles.
5. Tá sí ina ______________ i nDún nan Gall.
6. ?

PUZAL 4

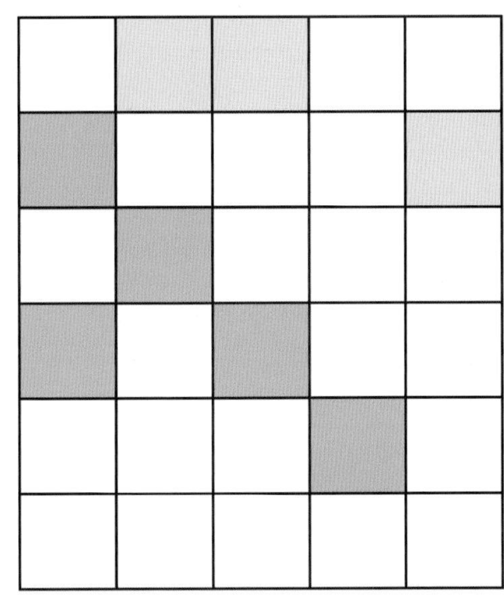

1. Déanaimid corpoideachas sa ______________ spóirt.
2. Cheannaigh mé bainne agus arán sa ______________ do mo mhamaí.
3. Aon chéad lúide fiche cothrom le ______________.
4. Titeann sneachta anuas ón ______________.
5. Bhí mé thuas staighre agus thit mé ______________.
6. ?

Freagraí ar leathanach 78

Recipe: Reindeer Pancakes

Reindeer pancakes make a hearty Christmas morning breakfast, and they're not too tough to prepare!

You will need:

- 300 g self-raising flour
- 1 tsp baking powder
- 1 tbsp caster sugar
- 2 medium eggs
- 300 ml milk
- Oil or butter for the pan
- Rashers/streaky bacon
- Sliced banana
- Chocolate chips or raisins
- Raspberries or strawberries

Equipment:

- Weighing scales
- Measuring jug
- Mixing bowl
- Sieve
- Whisk
- Oven tray
- Parchment paper
- Non-stick frying pan
- Selection of plates and cutlery

What to do:

1. Begin by weighing out ingredients for the batter.
2. Sieve the flour into a large bowl and add the baking powder and sugar. Crack in two eggs and whisk until smooth, adding the milk while whisking.
3. Grill bacon according to the instructions on the packet.
4. Turn the hob to a medium heat and add a splash of oil or small knob of butter to a non-stick frying pan. When it has heated, add batter according to the size of pancake you require. (Remember: to assemble reindeer pancakes, you will need some small and larger circular pancakes, and some longer, thin pancakes.)
5. Cook pancake until bubbles start to form on the surface, then flip over and cook on the other side.
6. Once the pancakes and bacon are finished cooking, gather the other reindeer components of your choice (banana, chocolate chip, etc.) and assemble some reindeer faces!
7. Serve and enjoy!

Be safe!
Ask an adult for help with using the oven and hob.

Sudoku 4

Have you done Sudoku 1, Sudoku 2 and Sudoku 3 on pages 14, 23 and 35? Try this final puzzle to prove you are a sudoku star!

			8				7	
	4	2				6	5	
9	6							
		9			6		2	
8	2			1			3	6
	3		2			9		
							9	5
	9	5				4	1	
	8				3			

Answers on page 79

ChristMaths Time!

It's time to take on the ChristMazes and ChristMaths challenges!
On your marks, get set, puzzle!

1. Can you help Santa to land his sleigh on the roof of the house?

2.

Use addition, subtraction and multiplication to complete each of the problems that make up these maths puzzles.

Answers on page 79

Forbairt Foclóra

An raibh a fhios agat nach bhfuil ach 18 litir in aibítir na Gaeilge? Seo chugat 18 focal nua ag tosú leis na litreacha sin chun do chuid Gaeilge a shaibhriú.

Amhrasach

Dubious/Questionable

'Bhí mé amhrasach faoin ríomhphost a fuair mé; cén fáth go mbeadh strainséir ag iarraidh airgead a thabhairt dom?'

Beoga

Vibrant/Lively

'Is ceantar beoga é cathair na Gaillimhe, bíonn rud éigin i gcónaí ar siúl ann.'

Casfhocal

Tongue twister

'Taitníonn an casfhocal faoi sicíní liom – seacht sicín ina seasamh sa sneachta lá sneachta.'

Dea-mhúinte

Polite/Well mannered

'Is duine dea-mhúinte í, deir sí i gcónaí "le do thoil" agus "go raibh maith agat".'

Easuan

Insomnia

'Tá brón orm gur thit mé i mo chodladh sa rang, a mhúinteoir. Tá easuan orm; níor chodail mé ar chor ar bith aréir.'

Frídíní

Germs

'Caith uait an ciarsúr sin, tá sé lán le frídíní!'

Gioblach

Dishevelled/Raggedy

'Tá an t-léine sin sean agus gioblach, caith sa bhosca bruscair é.'

Hurlamaboc

Commotion/Uproar

'Bhí hurlamaboc ann aréir nuair a bhuaigh Maigh Eo craobh na hÉireann.'

Imleacán
Belly button
'Bíonn babaithe ceangailte lena mamaithe tríd an imleacán.'

Luiteoga
Leggings
'Is maith liom luiteoga a chaitheamh faoi mo ghúna sa gheimhreadh.'

Nod
Hint
'Níl an freagra ar eolas agam, a mhúinteoir. Tabhair nod dom, le do thoil!'

Mairbhleach
Numb
'Tá sé ag cur sneachta. Tá mo mhéara mairbhleach leis an bhfuacht.'

Osna
Sigh
'Lig sé osna as nuair a d'éirigh leis an bhfoireann rugbaí úd a fháil sa nóiméad deireanach den chluiche.'

Pionsúirín
Tweezers
'Thit mé taobh amuigh agus d'úsáid mo mhamaí pionsúirín chun an t-adhmad a bhaint de mo lámha.'

Réchúiseach
Easy-going/Chilled
'Is duine réchúiseach mé; ní chuireann rud ar bith strus orm.'

Sos cogaidh
Ceasefire
'Ní ceart go mbeadh cogadh ann. Tá sos cogaidh uainn anois.'

Trangláilte
Cluttered
'Tá an seomra seo trangláilte. Tá mé chun go leor stuif a thabhairt go dtí an siopa carthanachta.'

Uaschamóg
Apostrophe
'Conas a litríon tú Aoife's? A-O-I-F-E-uaschamóg-S.'

The loved and pampered pets of the *Festival* offices are some of our furriest and best friends. We thought it was time the readers heard their stories.

Names: Binky and Emma

Breeds: Binky is a Harlequin Lop, and Emma is a Dutch rabbit!

Ages: 5 (Binky), 3 (Emma)

Special talents: Binky's special talent is his ability to jump super high into the air when he is excited. Fun fact: this is known as a 'binky', a word used to describe a rabbit's happy dance, which often occurs when a rabbit is very excited or enjoying themselves. This is where Binky got his name from!

Emma's special talent is her ability to sniff out a banana no matter where it is hidden in a room!

What are their stories? Binky was adopted from the DSPCA by Ruth at only two months old. He was so tiny when she brought him home, he could fit in the palm of her hand! While Binky loves human company, Ruth was worried he might be lonely, so she decided to adopt Emma from Rabbit Rescue Ireland. The pair immediately fell in love and have been inseparable ever since! Rabbits are extremely social creatures, and they really benefit from having a companion of their own kind. Binky and Emma spend a lot of time grooming each other, which is how rabbits communicate their affection for each other. The pair are indoor rabbits and are fully litterbox-trained (like a cat!). They are very curious, and enjoy running up and down the stairs, exploring every room in the house. They also love supervised playtime in the garden. Rabbits are fond of doing 'zoomies' when they are excited – just like dogs! Neither Binky nor Emma enjoy being picked up, because it frightens them; however, if a person sits down on the ground, the two of them will happily lounge beside them and enjoy head rubs. Binky will even hop onto his favourite humans' laps for a cuddle – if he's in the right mood! Their favourite foods are bananas and carrots; however, they can only have these in small amounts, as they will get an upset tummy if they eat too many treats! Most of their diet consists of fresh hay and dried pellets. After eating their breakfast, Binky and Emma will happily nap on the couch for hours!

Name: Po

Age: 6

Special talents: Catching flies.

What's his story? Carla's sister adopted Po when he was a kitten, but when he was two years old, she moved into a house where no pets were allowed (boo!), so he had to go and live with Carla instead. Now he and Carla are best friends. As a kitten, Po had an illness that left him with a type of arthritis in one of his paws and weakened his eyesight a little. But that doesn't stop him exploring the garden, eating catmint and chirruping at the birds. Po used to be too scared to go outside, but now he LOVES being out in the garden with Carla on a balmy summer evening, as well as belly rubs, snuggles and giving kisses on the nose. He HATES the hoover.

Name: Luna Belafonte

Breed: Jack Russell

Age: 14

Special talents: Protects her family from anyone trying to deliver post or parcels. At all costs. Catching bubbles. Accumulating a stash of sausages from the neighbours. Swimming in the Liffey. Evening zoomies.

What's her story? Laura got Luna when she was six months old as a friend for her other dog, Missy, but they soon became sisters. Luna's best friend in the world was a cat named Hugo, and though she has since become a big sister to two more cats, none of them are quite like Hugo, and she likes to remind them of that. When Luna was seven, she took a big flight to Canada and lived in Montreal for a year. She loved city life so much, and she even learned many dog-specific words in French so she could play with the other dogs at the park: 'saucisse' being the most important one. Since coming back to Ireland, Luna has become a big sister to two human siblings, and even though she's an old girl now, she loves nothing more than playing with them in the garden, especially when Mom and Dad bring out the bubble machine! It's a three-person job to catch all those pesky bubbles! She's the most loving and loyal girl, and Laura and her family feel very lucky that she came into their lives.

Name: Benny

Age: 4

Special talents: Keeping his fur super neat and clean. Giving the perfect 'Puss in Boots' eyes.

What's his story? Benny was adopted when he was only two months old by Isabelle and her family. Benny is an extremely energetic and playful cat and can always be found purring contently or looking for a chase around the house and the garden. He is a fantastic escape artist so his family have to be careful at night, because he will find any little hole or open window (no matter how small the gap) to squeeze out of. He is not the smartest of cats, and has often been seen running head first into walls, or yelling at birds before he chases them, giving them ample time to fly away. Benny doesn't have very many cat friends (they find him a bit overeager!) but he gets plenty of playtime, cuddles and kisses from his family to make up for it! He is very fussy about his fur, so much so that he refuses to wear a collar, and he spends most of his time cleaning and tidying it up so that he looks extra handsome at all times. Benny is often so excited to play that he doesn't realise how tired he gets, so needs to be put down for naps and tucked into bed at night. When he is not playing or escaping, he can be found cuddled in his favourite special cardboard box with his little fish toy.

Have you got an amazing pet? Send a photo and tell us about them (150 words max.) and they might be featured in next year's *Festival* annual. Remember to include their name, and their breed and age, if known. Ask a teacher, parent or guardian to email us at festival@educate.ie by 28 February 2025.

Christmas Calculations

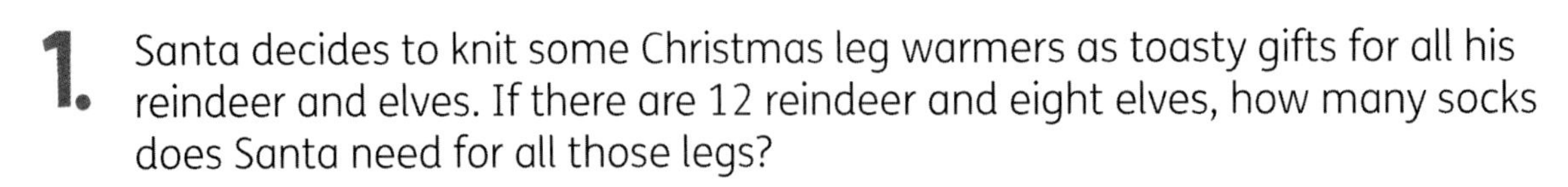

1. Santa decides to knit some Christmas leg warmers as toasty gifts for all his reindeer and elves. If there are 12 reindeer and eight elves, how many socks does Santa need for all those legs?

2. Mrs Claus is filling buckets of water for the reindeer to drink.

a. It takes three minutes to fill one bucket. How long will it take to fill 12 buckets?

b. If the 12 reindeer share each bucket of water between two, how many buckets will Mrs Claus need?

c. How long would it take to fill the new number of buckets?

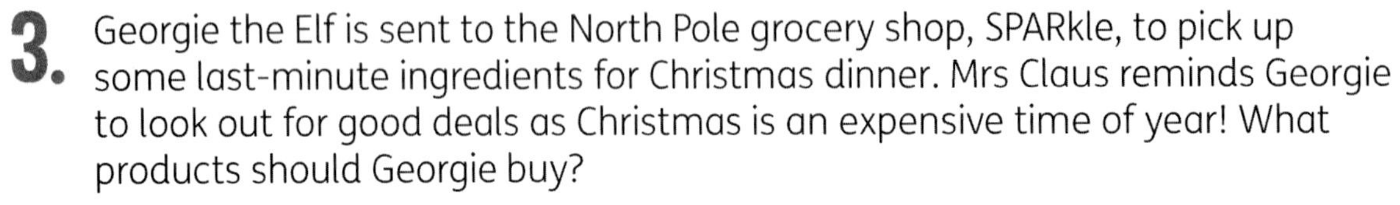

3. Georgie the Elf is sent to the North Pole grocery shop, SPARkle, to pick up some last-minute ingredients for Christmas dinner. Mrs Claus reminds Georgie to look out for good deals as Christmas is an expensive time of year! What products should Georgie buy?

a. 500 g of cranberry sauce for €1, or 600 g of cranberry sauce for €1.25?

b. A 10 kg turkey for €10, or a 12 kg turkey for €11?

c. Two single 100 g blocks of jelly at 60 c each, or a double packet for €1?

d. A bag of ten oranges for €1.70, or two bags of six oranges for €1.20 each?

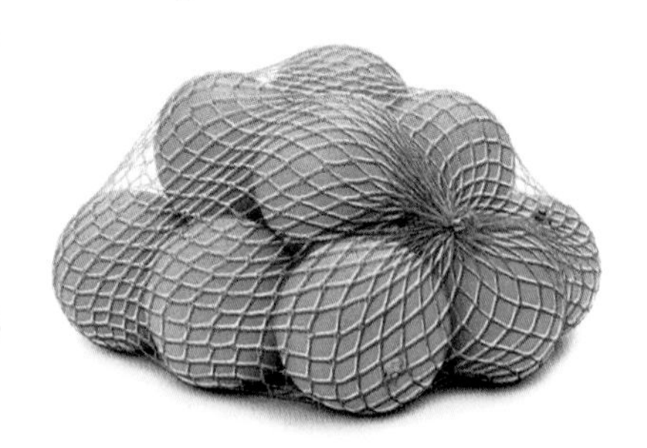

Tip! To work out the best value, work out a unit price you can compare. If 500 g of cranberry sauce is €1, how much is 100 g? If 600 g of cranberry sauce is €1.25, how much is 100 g? Which is better?

4. Fifth Class are planning to hold a Christmas market in the school hall. They must decide how many stalls can fit in the hall.

- Each stallholder will get a table measuring 1 metre wide x 2 metres long.
- The school hall measures 30 metres x 30 metres.

If they place the tables in rows and they must leave 1 metre of space around each table on all sides, what is the maximum number of stalls they can host?

Consider drawing the problem to help you work it out. Use grid paper and decide that each side of a square represents 1 metre. Draw the school hall first, before adding any tables!

5. The Czompa family live in Spain. They are travelling home to Ireland for Christmas.

- The drive from their house to Málaga Airport takes 35 minutes.
- It takes 1 hour and 16 minutes to check in their luggage, travel through security and walk to their gate.
- They arrive at their gate at 11.01 a.m., but their flight does not board until 11.47 a.m.
- Their flight takes off at 12 p.m. and lands at Dublin Airport at 3.05 p.m. (Spanish time).
- It takes another two hours to leave the plane, claim their bags and travel to their family home.

Spain is in a different time zone to Ireland so there is a time difference between the two countries – Ireland is one hour behind Spain. Make sure to take this into account in your calculations!

a. What time did they leave their house in Spain?
b. What time (Irish time) did they arrive at their family home in Ireland?
c. How long was the Czompas' total journey?

Answers on page 79

Recipe as Gaeilge: Crann Nollag Crispíní Rís

Comhábhair:

- 300 g seacláid
- 150 g crispíní rís

Le maisiú:

- 100 g seacláid
- Smarties nó M&M's dearga agus glasa
- Siúcra reoáin

Uirlisí cócaireachta:

- Párpháipéar bácála
- Rialóir agus peann luaidhe
- Scálaí cistine
- Babhla measctha
- Sáspan
- Spadal
- Taespúnóg
- Pláta
- Criathar

Treoracha:

1. Leag an párpháipéar bácála amach ar an mbord agus bain úsáide as an rialóir agus an peann luaidhe chun ocht gcros a tharraingt ar thomhais éagsúla – 22 cm, 20 cm, 18 cm, 16 cm, 14 cm, 12 cm, 10 cm agus 8 cm.

2. Leáigh an 300 g seacláid i mbabhla mór thar pota uisce beirithe.

3. Doirt na crispíní rís isteach sa bhabhla agus measc leis an seacláid iad.
4. Ag baint úsáide as taespúnóg, leag na crispíní rís seacláide amach ar na crosa ar an bpárpháipéar bácála.
5. Más mian leat, is féidir leat iad a mhaisiú le Smarties nó M&M's dearga agus glasa!
6. Lig do na crosa ar fad fuarú GO HIOMLÁN.
7. Leáigh an 100 g seacláid i mbabhla beag thar pota uisce beirithe.
8. Cuir an chros is mó ar phláta mór.
9. Úsáid an seacláid leáite ar nós gliú chun na crosa a greamú dá chéile. Tosaigh leis an gceann is mó ag an mbun agus cuir seacláid leáite i lár na croise agus leag an chéad chros eile rothlaithe ar a bharr.
10. Lean ar aghaidh ag greamú agus ag rothlú na gcros go dtí go bhfuil gach cros úsáidte agus cruth crann Nollag déanta agat.
11. Criathraigh an siúcra reoáin ar bharr an chrainn ar nós sneachta.
12. Bain sult as!

FOCLÓIR

Párpháipéar bácála – baking parchment
Siúcra reoáin – icing sugar
Cros – cross
Uisce beirithe – boiling water
Rothlaithe – rotated
Criathraigh – sieve

IRELAND'S CHEERLEADERS

Cheer sport, also known as cheerleading, is one of the fastest-growing sports for young people in Ireland and around the world. It even became a recognised Olympic Games sport in 2021. There are many kinds of teams, from novices who take part for entertainment and fun, to elite athletes who take part in competitions or even work as cheerleaders or cheerleading coaches.

You may have seen cheerleading in films. Cheerleaders are often shown performing routines and showcasing amazing dance and movement skills on the sidelines of other sports, such as American football, to hype up the crowd. However, cheer is a sport in its own right and is not just performed on the sidelines. Cheerleaders have their own elite competitions.

In Ireland, there are cheer clubs in counties including Dublin, Wicklow, Kerry and Galway. Cheerleaders can also try out with the national body, Cheer Sport Ireland, if they want to represent Ireland in international competitions.

Team Ireland has taken part in the International Cheer Union World Championships each year since 2021. This year, a documentary called *Eat/Sleep/Cheer/Repeat* was released. It was filmed in 2021 and followed Team Ireland as they prepared for and travelled to the World Cheerleading Championships in Florida. In 2022, Team Ireland placed 9th in the world in the Coed Elite Division, returning the following year to hold their place in the top ten with a 10th-place ranking. That year, 2023, also saw Team Ireland's Junior Hip Hop team finish 8th in the world in their division! Not bad, considering the International Cheerleading Union has 120 member countries!

Cheerleading is often seen as a sport for girls, but anyone can take part. Important skills for cheer include strength and teamwork. Not all cheerleaders perform the same job on the team. For example, those who are thrown in the air are known as flyers, while the people who hold, throw and catch are known as bases.

INTERESTING FACTS ABOUT CHEERLEADING

- Cheerleading started out in the United States as an all-male sport! Organised cheerleading began at universities in the late 1800s, but female students did not take part until the 1920s.
- Like many sports, cheerleading can be dangerous and can carry a high serious injury rate for female athletes. Inclusion and team spirit are important when working together to practise and perform stunting and pyramid techniques in particular.
- Professional cheerleading began in the 1950s. This was also the time when the US National Cheerleaders Association was formed.
- In the 1960s, rankings and organised cheerleading competitions began.
- The 1980s are seen as the beginning of 'modern cheerleading', as stunts and gymnastics were introduced into cheer routines.

Find Your CHEER NAME!

Find the first part of your nickname by using the first letter of your first name. Find the second part of your nickname by using the month of your birth. For example, if your name is Danielle and you were born in February, your nickname is Happy Flyer. If your name is Paul and you were born in September, your nickname is Top Stomp.

A – Bubbly
B – Merry
C – Hyper
D – Happy
E – Awesome
F – Joy
G – Peppy
H – Sweet
I – Dazzling
J – Fierce
K – Bliss
L – Power
M – Gleeful
N – Sunny
O – Stellar
P – Top
Q – Cool
R – Bonny
S – Super
T – Jazzy
U – Brave
V – Bold
W – Lucky
X – Hale
Y – Daring
Z – Heart

January – Tumble
February – Flyer
March – Pom Pom
April – Jump
May – Spirit
June – Roller
July – Chant
August – Clap
September – Stomp
October – Punch
November – Shake
December – Thrill

My name is: ______________________

But my friends call me: ______________________

My shoe size is: ______________________

My height is: ______________________

My favourite song this year is: ______________________

My top three memories of 2024 are:

1. ______________________

2. ______________________

3. ______________________

My favourite movie was: ______________________

My favourite snack is: ______________________

My favourite way to spend time is: ______________________

I couldn't live without: ______________________

The best book I read was: ______________________

Three words to describe my year are:

1. ______________________

2. ______________________

3. ______________________

My advice to my 2025 self is:

____

____

____

All I want for Christmas is: ______________________

Nathanna Nollag

An bhfuil an foclóir a bhaineann leis an Nollaig ar eolas agat? An féidir leat na ceisteanna seo faoin Nollaig a fhreagairt? An féidir leat na freagraí a aimsiú sa chuardach focal?

1. An rud ina mbíonn Daidí na Nollag ag suí nuair a bhíonn sé ag eitilt timpeall an domhain Oíche Nollag.

   _ _ _ _   _ _ _ _ _ _ _ _ _ _

2. An t-éan a itear go traidisiúnta ag béile na Nollag.

   _ _ _ _ _ _

3. An figiúr a dhéanann páistí as an rud bán a thiteann ón spéir.

   _ _ _ _   _ _ _ _ _ _ _ _

4. Bíonn an duine beag seo ag cabhrú le Daidí na Nollag na bréagáin a dhéanmh sa Mhol Thuaidh.

   _ _ _ _ _ _ _ _ _ _ _ _

5. An dá rud is coitianta le cur ag barr crann Nollag.

   _ _ _ _ _ _ agus _ _ _ _ _ _ _

6. Na hamhráin a chantar ag an Nollaig.

   _ _ _ _ _ _

7. Fágann páistí iad seo amach Oíche Nollag, ag súil go mbeidh siad líonta maidin Nollag.

   _ _ _ _ _ _   _ _ _ _ _ _

8. Tagann Daidí na Nollag anuas an rud seo i do theach.

   _ _ _ _ _ _ _

9. Na rudaí daite a chuirtear ar an gcrann Nollag.

   _ _ _ _ _ _ _ _ _ _ _

10. An t-ainm ar an leanbh a bhí ag Muire agus Iósaf.

    _ _ _ _

11. Tugtar iad seo dá chéile Lá Nollag. De ghnáth, bíonn siad clúdaithe le páipéar daite.

    _ _ _ _ _ _ _ _ _ _ _

12. Tá ocht gcinn de na hainmhithe seo ag Daidí na Nollag. Is féidir leo eitilt.

    _ _ _ _ _ _ _ _

13. Milseog thraidisiúnta a bhíonn ann tar éis dinnéar na Nollag. Uaireanta bíonn sí trí thine.

    _ _ _ _ _   _ _ _ _ _ _

14. An rud glas a bhíonn i do theach um Nollag. Cuirtear soilse agus rudaí daite air.

    _ _ _ _ _   _ _ _ _ _ _

T	U	R	C	A	Í	S	P	O	R	T	S	C	M
B	L	Ú	B	N	O	L	L	G	I	É	R	A	O
R	F	E	A	R	S	N	E	A	C	H	T	A	P
O	S	H	Í	E	A	L	U	C	H	A	R	T	C
N	C	A	M	S	U	Ó	L	O	S	P	M	Á	H
N	R	C	R	A	N	N	N	O	L	L	A	G	A
I	L	B	R	O	N	N	T	A	N	A	I	S	G
O	U	R	É	I	N	A	G	M	H	M	S	R	S
S	C	N	A	I	N	G	E	A	L	A	I	C	T
L	H	P	Ó	G	S	N	E	A	C	R	Ú	O	O
Á	A	G	C	E	I	A	I	N	L	Ó	C	L	C
T	R	H	A	A	M	T	S	Ó	D	G	H	L	A
C	A	R	R	S	L	E	A	M	H	N	Á	I	N
R	C	E	Ú	R	É	A	L	T	A	O	I	G	O
A	H	T	I	Í	A	C	R	Ó	L	L	N	S	L
N	Á	Ó	L	E	R	B	H	U	C	L	A	I	L
G	N	L	R	É	I	N	F	H	I	A	R	É	A
L	C	R	A	N	O	L	L	N	A	G	P	Á	G

Freagraí ar leathanaigh 79 agus 80

Crack the Crackers

Can you solve the riddles in these Christmas crackers?

Of all of Santa's reindeer
I'm the fastest one
My first is in deer
My last is in run
Who am I?

They chop me down
To dress me up
I drink lots of water
But not from a cup
What am I?

I'm a catchy carol
About a melty guy
I wave goodbye
Saying don't you cry
When I have to go away
What am I?

I plant the idea
When people show love
When there's kisses
below
I am above
What am I?

Answers on page 80

Count and Colour

How many of each of the following items can you find in this cluttered Christmas picture?

Colour them in and count them as you find them, then see if you were correct by checking the answer at the back of the book.

- Stars
- Baubles
- Gingerbread men
- Lights
- Candles
- Snow globes
- Hats
- Bows
- Wreaths
- Gift sacks
- Cups
- Bells

Answers on page 80

THE COUNTY CROSSWORD

Do you know your Irish counties? Solve the clues below to complete this bumper county crossword.

DOWN

1. This county is home to towns such as Edgeworthstown and Granard. (8)
2. This county is the birthplace of the poet Patrick Kavanagh and the rugby player Tommy Bowe. (8)
4. This county is home to the Cliffs of Moher and the Burren. (5)
6. This county contains Leinster's only Gaeltacht areas, Ráth Chairn near Athboy, and Baile Ghib near Navan. (5)
7. The very centre of Ireland, located on the shore of Lough Ree, is found in this county. (9)
9. This Munster county is the home of the Rose of Tralee competition. (5)
10. One of only two counties never to win an All-Ireland Championship in any Gaelic game, the other being Wicklow. (9)
11. The area where this county is located is known as 'the Déise'. (9)
13. Parts of this coastal county, such as Strandhill, are well known for surfing. (5)
16. An area of this county, Ratheniska, has been home to the National Ploughing Championships in recent years. (5)
17. This county includes towns such as Coleraine and Limevady. (5)
21. This Ulster county contains sights such as the Giant's Causeway. (6)
22. This county is well known for sports, including winning the GAA All-Ireland Senior Football Championship four times since the year 2000, most recently in 2021. (6)
27. The largest town in this county is Tullamore. (6)
30. Ireland's smallest county. (5)

ACROSS

3. This county is known as 'the Garden of Ireland'. (7)
5. Rugby is popular in this Munster county, with teams such as Garryowen and UL Bohemians. (8)
8. This county is known as 'the Lakeland County' as it is reputed to be home to 365 lakes. (5)
9. This county's GAA teams are known as the Lilywhites. (7)
12. This county is home to towns such as Mullingar, Moate and Kilbeggan. (9)
14. Well-known people from this county include Micheál Martin, Marty Morrissey and Roy Keane. (4)
15. Ireland's largest island, Achill, lies off the coast of this county. (4)
16. This county has the lowest population in the country. (6)
18. The River Barrow flows through this landlocked county, which is also, along with Wexford, home to the Blackstairs Mountains. (6)
19. *The Late Late Show* presenter Patrick Kielty hails from this county. (4)
20. This Ulster county is known as 'the Orchard County' because of its many apple orchards. (6)
23. This county includes towns such as Letterkenny, Buncrana and Lifford. (7)
24. The largest landlocked county in Ireland. Famous faces from this county include the 2 Johnnies, Babs Keating and Roz Purcell. (9)
25. This county is technically now divided into three counties including Fingal and Dún Laoghaire-Rathdown. (6)
26. The largest county in Leinster, home to towns such as Enniscorthy and Bunclody. (7)
28. Well-known people from this county include YouTuber Seán William McLoughlin (jacksepticeye) and actress Nicola Coughlan. (6)
29. Railway stations in this county are called MacDonagh and Thomastown. (8)

Answers on page 80

Festival

Christmas Writing Competition

Here at *Festival*, we know how much fun it is to think up Christmas tales and spend time inventing and writing interesting characters and plots, so we would like to invite you to try it!

Would you like to see your writing appear in *Festival* and maybe win a book token to get your 2025 reading off to an epic start? Then read on ...

1. The *Festival* writing competition is open to Fifth and Sixth Class students.
2. Entry format: A poem or a story (fiction or non-fiction) of 300–1,000 words.
3. All entries must be submitted as an email attachment, such as a Microsoft Word document, with your name, school and the name of your story in the file name.
4. Submit to: festival@educate.ie by 31 January 2025. Entries must be submitted by an adult who is responsible for you, such as a parent or guardian. If your entry is successful, *Festival* will need to get in touch to let you know that you have won and to arrange your prize. We can **only** do this by contacting **an adult**.
5. A winner will be chosen and announced by the end of April 2025. They will receive a prize and their entry will appear in *Festival* 2025.
6. Runners-up may be chosen to receive runner-up prizes and appear in *Festival* 2025.

What will you write about?

Remember to ask yourself who, what, when, where and why in order to come up with your Christmas plot. Describe the characters and the places they visit. Try using the senses – what are the sights, sounds and smells they encounter? Think about emotions – how do the characters feel? Joyful? Sad? Confused?

Consider the issues you have learned about in this year's *Festival*. Were you inspired by reading about anniversaries to include an event or celebration in your story? Has reading about celebrities such as Jürgen Klopp and Daniel Wiffen or discovering Ireland's cheerleaders given you an idea to use some element of sport or competition in your plot? Could you incorporate some new words you learned in our Amazing Words article? Maybe you could look up some fantastic words that the team here at *Festival* have never heard of!

After conquering Cluedle, Sumoji, Crack the Crackers and Sudoku, could you add a puzzle or mystery element to your story?

Inspiration can come from anywhere. Wherever yours comes from, all that is important is to enjoy the process of creating your story.

Have fun and good luck!

ANSWERS

Page 5: 2024 Quiz

1. Dragon
2. Sky
3. France
4. Simon Harris
5. Kansas City Chiefs
6. Travis Kelce
7. *The Tortured Poets Department*
8. *The Polar Express*
9. *The Gruffalo*
10. Jason Smyth
11. Dua Lipa
12. *Bluey*
13. Jordie Barrett
14. Olly Murs
15. Ant and Dec
16. *Man Up?*
17. Cillian Murphy
18. Billie Eilish
19. 15c
20. *Monopoly*
21. Wexford
22. Mary Robinson
23. Toulouse
24. False: Manchester City were beaten by Manchester United in the FA Cup final.

Page 7: Spot the Difference 1

Page 10: Synonym Rolls!

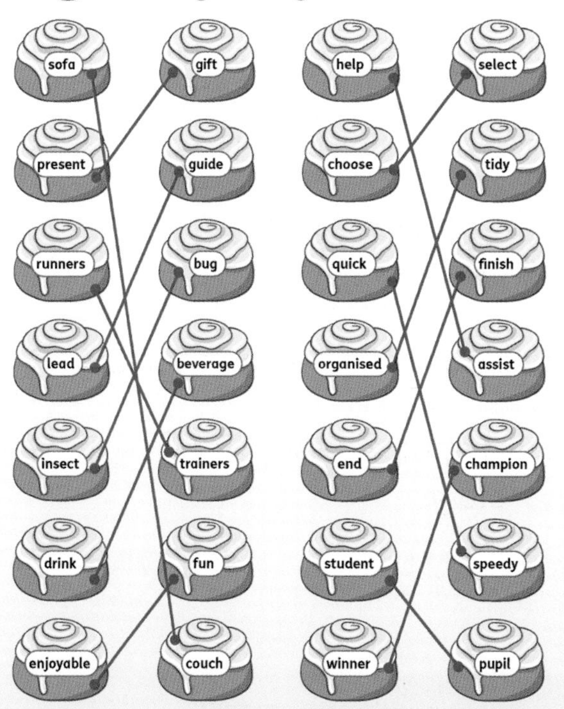

Page 11: Synonym Rolls as Gaeilge!

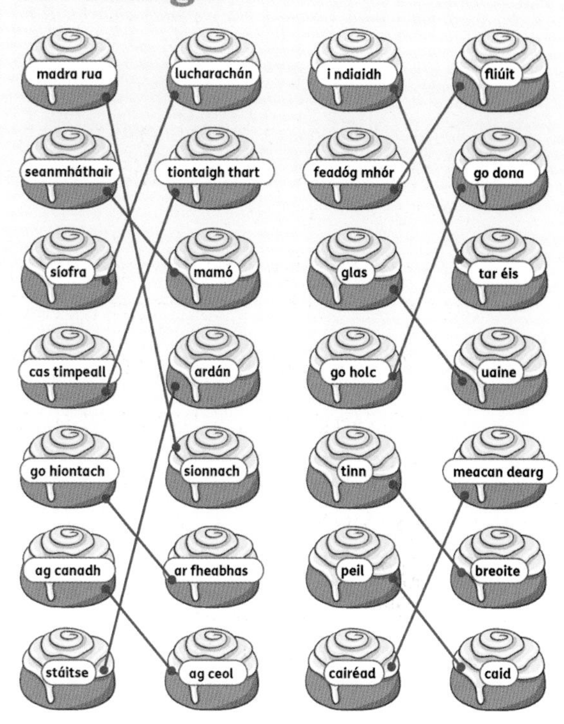

Page 14: Sudoku 1

3	2	4	5	6	1	7	8	9
1	9	8	4	2	7	6	3	5
7	5	6	3	8	9	4	1	2
8	7	5	6	1	3	2	9	4
2	6	3	7	9	4	8	5	1
9	4	1	8	5	2	3	6	7
5	8	2	9	4	6	1	7	3
4	3	9	1	7	8	5	2	6
6	1	7	2	3	5	9	4	8

Page 15: Tráth na gCeist: Cé hlad?

1. Nicola Coughlan
2. Jude Bellingham
3. Ariana Grande
4. Kai Cenat
5. Luke Littler

Page 22: Aimsigh na Difríochtaí 2

Page 23: Sudoku 2

6	9	8	3	4	1	5	7	2
2	5	1	7	8	9	3	4	6
4	7	3	5	6	2	1	9	8
8	3	9	1	5	4	2	6	7
1	2	7	6	9	8	4	5	3
5	4	6	2	7	3	8	1	9
7	6	2	8	1	5	9	3	4
3	1	4	9	2	6	7	8	5
9	8	5	4	3	7	6	2	1

Page 29: Spot the Difference 3

Page 35: Sudoku 3

2	9	3	5	4	7	6	8	1
1	5	4	8	2	6	7	3	9
6	7	8	3	9	1	2	4	5
4	1	7	2	6	3	9	5	8
3	2	5	1	8	9	4	7	6
8	6	9	7	5	4	3	1	2
7	8	1	9	3	2	5	6	4
5	4	2	6	7	8	1	9	3
9	3	6	4	1	5	8	2	7

Page 48: Sumoji!

1. Gingerbread men = 5, stars = 2, santas = 3; 25.
2. Snowflakes = 4, reindeer = 6, sleighs = 1; 11.
3. Baubles = 7, bows = 8, snowmen = 9; 48.
4. Gifts = 2, holly = 5, puddings = 4; 110.
5. Elves = 7, candy canes = 3, stockings = 9; 38.
6. Trees = 4, holly = 2, gifts = 7; 448.

Page 50: Cluedle!

Puzzle 1

1. EIGHT
2. STEAM
3. KAYAK
4. LIMBO
5. YEAST
6. STYLE

Puzzle 2

1. HABIT
2. JUICE
3. SPOON
4. SCALP
5. TREAT
6. JAPAN

Puzzle 3

1. EAGLE
2. ADULT
3. BLIND
4. MONTH
5. PHOTO
6. AGENT

Puzzle 4

1. TEXAS
2. TRAIN
3. BLUSH
4. COACH
5. ARROW
6. WATCH

Page 52: Cluedle as Gaeilge!

Puzal 1

1. DEICH
2. NÁDÚR
3. DUAIS
4. PEATA
5. CÚIRT
6. PÁIRC

Puzal 2

1. MAMAÍ
2. DEOCH
3. GORTA
4. NÓCHA
5. FIDIL
6. FOCAL

Puzal 3

1. LITIR
2. CLOCH
3. MILIS
4. DRUMA
5. CÓNAÍ
6. CLUAS

Puzal 4

1. HALLA
2. SIOPA
3. OCHTÓ
4. SPÉIR
5. ANUAS
6. SCÉAL

Page 55: Sudoku 4

5	1	3	8	6	4	2	7	9
7	4	2	9	3	1	6	5	8
9	6	8	7	2	5	3	4	1
4	5	9	3	8	6	1	2	7
8	2	7	4	1	9	5	3	6
6	3	1	2	5	7	9	8	4
3	7	6	1	4	2	8	9	5
2	9	5	6	7	8	4	1	3
1	8	4	5	9	3	7	6	2

Page 56: ChristMaths Time!

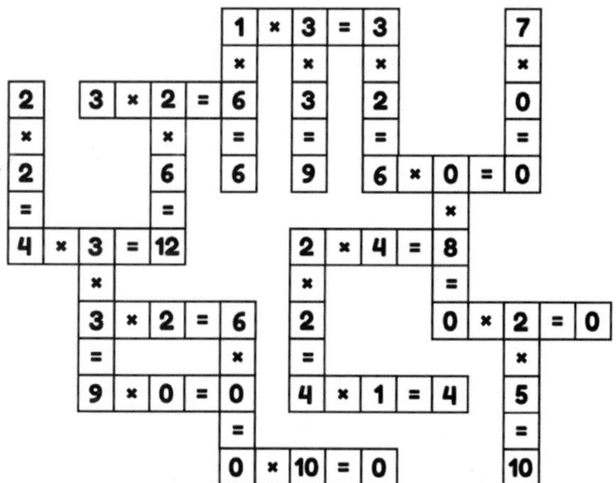

Page 62: Christmas Calculations

1. 64 [12 reindeer with four legs each = 48. 8 elves with two legs each = 16. 48 + 16 = 64].
2. a. 3 x 12 = 36 minutes; b. 12 / 2 = 6 buckets; c. 3 x 6 = 18 minutes.
3. a. 500 g of cranberry sauce for €1;
   b. A 12 kg turkey for €11;
   c. A double packet of jelly for €1;
   d. A bag of 10 oranges for €1.70.
4. 70 [10 rows of 7 stalls].
5. a. 9.10 a.m.; b. 4.05 p.m.; c. 7 hours 55 minutes.

Page 70: Nathanna Nollag

1. CARR SLEAMHNÁIN
2. TURCAÍ
3. FEAR SNEACHTA
4. LUCHARACHÁN
5. RÉALTA agus AINGEAL
6. CARÚIL
7. STOCA NOLLAG
8. SIMLÉAR
9. MAISIÚCHÁIN
10. ÍOSA
11. BRONNTANAIS
12. RÉINFHIA
13. MARÓG NOLLAG
14. CRANN NOLLAG

Page 71: Nathanna Nollag

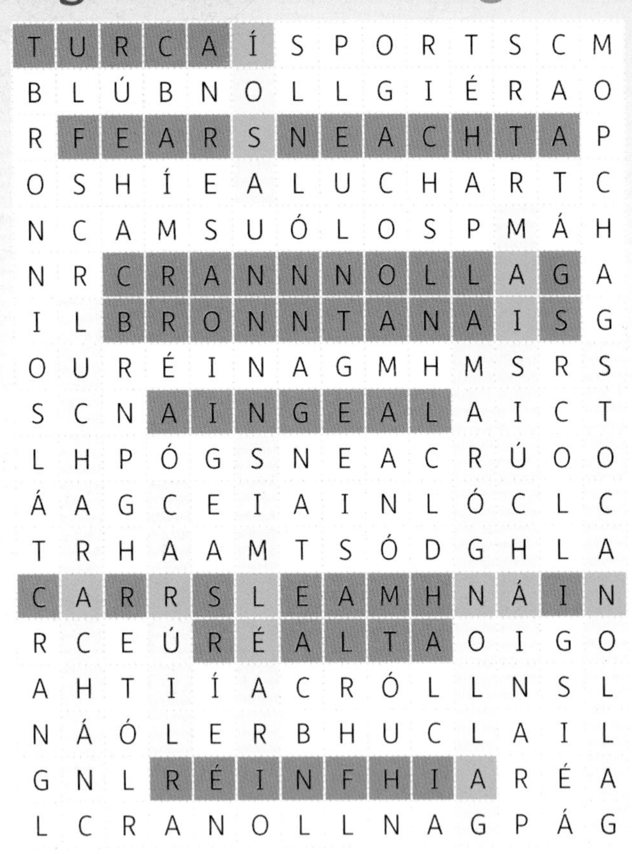

T	U	R	C	A	Í	S	P	O	R	T	S	C	M
B	L	Ú	B	N	O	L	L	G	I	É	R	A	O
R	F	E	A	R	S	N	E	A	C	H	T	A	P
O	S	H	Í	E	A	L	U	C	H	A	R	T	C
N	C	A	M	S	U	Ó	L	O	S	P	M	Á	H
N	R	C	R	A	N	N	N	O	L	L	A	G	A
I	L	B	R	O	N	N	T	A	N	A	I	S	G
O	U	R	É	I	N	A	G	M	H	M	S	R	S
S	C	N	A	I	N	G	E	A	L	A	I	C	T
L	H	P	Ó	G	S	N	E	A	C	R	Ú	O	O
Á	A	G	C	E	I	A	I	N	L	Ó	C	L	C
T	R	H	A	A	M	T	S	Ó	D	G	H	L	A
C	A	R	R	S	L	E	A	M	H	N	Á	I	N
R	C	E	Ú	R	É	A	L	T	A	O	I	G	O
A	H	T	I	Í	A	C	R	Ó	L	L	N	S	L
N	Á	Ó	L	E	R	B	H	U	C	L	A	I	L
G	N	L	R	É	I	N	F	H	I	A	R	É	A
L	C	R	A	N	O	L	L	N	A	G	P	Á	G

Page 72: Crack the Crackers

1. Dasher
2. A Christmas tree
3. The Christmas song 'Frosty the Snowman'
4. Mistletoe

Page 73: Count and Colour

- 12 Stars
- 8 Baubles
- 5 Gingerbread men
- 8 Lights
- 10 Candles
- 4 Snow globes
- 7 Hats
- 11 Bows
- 10 Wreaths
- 5 Gift sacks
- 9 Cups
- 7 Bells

Page 74: The County Crossword